THE FOUNDATION OF BRITISH EAST AFRICA

Photo by] SOMALI TRIBESMEN. [*Russell & Sons.*

THE FOUNDATION OF BRITISH EAST AFRICA

By J. W. Gregory, D.Sc

NEGRO UNIVERSITIES PRESS
NEW YORK

Originally published in 1901
by Horace Marshall & Son, London

Reprinted 1969 by
Negro Universities Press
A Division of Greenwood Publishing Corp.
New York

SBN 8371-1727-5

printed in united states of america

Preface

BRITISH East Africa has a threefold history, geographical, political and administrative, dealing respectively with the story of its exploration, the struggle for its possession and the beginning of its commercial development. These three histories relate to such different subjects that it is not easy to combine them into a connected story; but I have tried to tell as much of each as is necessary to explain the adventurous history of British East Africa from the voyages of the ancient merchants and Arab traders to the establishment of British rule.

Among the modern expeditions I have only described those which have had an important influence on the founding of British East Africa. The story of the expeditions which mapped the rivers, explored the branch roads, filled in the topographical details and determined the main features in the natural history and geology of the country, as well as of the journeys of the sportsmen who have opened up new ground, belongs to the geographical history of East Africa. It will record the discoveries of, amongst others, Ainsworth, Ansorge, Austin, Chanler, Delamere, Dundas, Hall, Hobley, von Höhnel, Mackinder, Moore, Neumann, Pigott, Scott-Elliot, Donaldson Smith, Eric Smith, Captain Smith, and the important contributions of the missionaries to our knowledge of the geography and ethnography.

I have however included a sketch of the early history of British East Africa; for it was the work of the classical traders whose stories threw over the country the glamour of myth and mystery, and of the mediaeval Portuguese travellers who showed its commercial value to Europe as a station on the route to India, that gave the country its fascination to the modern missionaries and geographical pioneers; and in turn it was their account of the pathos of native life and the horrors of the slave trade which inspired the political travellers whose work led to the establishment of British rule.

I have tried to tell the principal events in the three chief stages in the history of the country closing with the appointment in 1899 of Sir Harry Johnston as Commissioner of Uganda. From his work in Uganda great things were expected, for it is generally understood that he was sent out primarily as an African expert to advise as to the future administration of the country. This administration has been marked by some important reforms, but the test of his work will be his final report as to the requirements and resources of the country.

Since the manuscript was concluded, news of the mutiny in Somaliland and the deplorable death of Mr. Jenner, whose tact and integrity as chief judge at Mombasa did so much to establish native faith in British justice, and the rebellion in Nandi show that British East Africa has not yet secured the peace which is essential to that growth of population which is the country's greatest need.

These wars are most regrettable from financial as well as other considerations. The government of British East Africa will for some years inevitably be very costly. A cheap administration at the present stage must come to evil. Five millions of pounds are being spent on the Uganda railway, which will assuredly prove a bad investment if money for the development of the country be unwisely stinted. A more generous grant for the investigation of the economic resources of the country is especially necessary.

The present heavy expenditure in South Africa may lead to a reduction in the subsidy to British East

PREFACE

Africa; but no one who knows the country will doubt that undue economy now will cost dearly in the end. The administration of the adjoining state of German East Africa in many respects has set an example that might be copied with advantage.

As the book is popular in its scope I have not burdened it with references. The principal literature up to 1896 is referred to in my *Great Rift Valley*; after that date there is a complete record in the monthly summaries of literature by Dr. H. R. Mill and Mr. Heawood in the *Geographical Journal*. A catalogue of the blue books and other official publications is given in Messrs. P. S. King & Son's annual lists.

In conclusion I have to express my thanks to Mrs. Chaplain, who owing to my absence from England has kindly seen the book through the press; also to my colleague, Prof. Tucker, for his translation of the passage on the East Coast of Africa in the *Periplus*, and for some suggestive notes thereon.

J. W. GREGORY.

University, Melbourne.
May, 1901.

Contents

Chapter I
THE GEOGRAPHY OF BRITISH EAST AFRICA . . 3

Chapter II
THE NATIVES OF BRITISH EAST AFRICA . . . 17

Chapter III
THE DAWN OF EAST AFRICAN GEOGRAPHY . . 27
APPENDIX TO CHAPTER III: ACCOUNT OF THE EAST AFRICAN COAST IN "THE PERIPLUS OF THE RED SEA," TRANSLATED BY PROFESSOR TUCKER 49

Chapter IV
THE MOMBASA MISSIONS 52

Chapter V
THE QUEST FOR THE NILE SOURCES 71

Chapter VI
THE UGANDA ROAD AND THE TRAVERSE OF MASAILAND 81

CONTENTS

Chapter VII
STANLEY AND THE UGANDA MISSION 103

Chapter VIII
THE BRITISH EAST AFRICA COMPANY AND THE STRUGGLE FOR WITU 123

Chapter IX
THE MAZRUI REBELLION AND EMIGRATION . . 144

Chapter X
HOW THE MISSIONARIES RETURNED TO UGANDA . 162

Chapter XI
HOW LUGARD SAVED UGANDA. 174

Chapter XII
UGANDA UNDER THE FOREIGN OFFICE. . . . 199

Chapter XIII
THE FUTURE OF BRITISH EAST AFRICA . . . 237

List of Illustrations

SOMALI TRIBESMEN	*Frontispiece*	
THE BAOBAB TREE	*Facing p.*	8
IVORY TRADERS IN MASAI DRESS	,,	20
DR. LUDWIG KRAPF	,,	54
MASAI WARRIORS	,,	82
HENRY M. STANLEY, AT THE TIME OF HIS FIRST EXPLORATIONS IN AFRICA	,,	106
A GROUP OF UGANDA NATIVES	,,	112
ZANZIBAR NATIVES: GATHERING CLOVES	,,	128
MOMBASA	,,	146
FORT MOMBASA	,,	160
GENERAL F. D. LUGARD	,,	176
THE UGANDA RAILWAY: MAKUPA BRIDGE	,,	200
THE UGANDA RAILWAY: SCENERY NEAR VOI STATION	,,	224
THE UGANDA RAILWAY: CLEARING FOR MOMBASA STATION	,,	240
THE UGANDA RAILWAY: A STEEP GRADIENT	,,	248

MAPS

SANSON D'ABBEVILLE'S MAP OF EQUATORIAL AFRICA	,,	48
MAP OF BRITISH EAST AFRICA	*At end of volume*	

BOOK I

Chapter I

HE GEOGRAPHY OF BRITISH EAST AFRICA

"Geography is three-fourths of war."—*Von Moltke.*

THE British territories on the mainland of Eastern Equatorial Africa include about half a million square miles of country, extending from the shore of the Indian Ocean to the basin of the Nile. This vast area, more than four times the size of England and Wales, was acquired for the Empire by a company of merchants and philanthropists, known as the British East African Association. Their dominions were called British East Africa, a name still used in its original sense by geographers, though politicians now restrict it to a part of the eastern half of that area.

The inland boundaries of British East Africa, using the name in its geographical sense, are either artificial or uncertain. On the south, the British territories are separated from German East Africa by a line drawn from the coast at the port of Wanga, in a north-westerly direction, to the shore of the Victoria Nyanza; whence the boundary runs westward, along the first parallel of south latitude, till it reaches the Congo Free State. Except for a bend which gives Kilima Njaro, the highest of African mountains, to Germany, the southern frontier has been drawn straight across the country with diplomatic indifference to geographical features.

The north-eastern frontier is formed by the Juba, which makes a natural boundary up to the confluence of its chief head streams; but beyond that point it is perhaps uncertain which of the branches is the Juba of the diplomatist.

The northern boundary is the least definite, for Menelik, the "Emperor of Ethiopia," claims dominion over large portions of the lowlands to the south and west of the Abyssinian plateau, although they are included within the British sphere.

West of Abyssinia, British East Africa meets the old Equatorial provinces of Egypt, now under the joint protection of England and Egypt; but where the English sphere ends and the Anglo-Egyptian condominion begins is, as yet, a little vague.

So far as the limits can at present be drawn, British East Africa extends in length for some eight hundred and forty miles from south-east to north-west, with an average width of five hundred and sixty miles. It thus includes about five hundred thousand square miles. Politically, the country is divided into three parts—the Uganda Protectorate, which includes as much of the

Nile Basin and the Great Rift Valley as falls within the British sphere; the British East Africa Protectorate, which extends from the eastern wall of the Great Rift Valley to a line ten miles west of the Indian Ocean shore; and the Zanzibar Protectorate, which includes the islands of Zanzibar and Pemba, and a ten-mile belt along the coast. Geographically and historically, however, the three divisions on the mainland are one, and their permanent political separation is improbable.

Some knowledge of the physical geography of British East Africa is necessary in order to understand its recent history, for peculiar geographical conditions have rendered its administration especially difficult and interesting. The British colonisation of America and Australia began with the establishment of stations on the coast, whence settlements crept backward, step by step, up the chief river valleys, or along the main trade routes to the interior. The British conquest of India followed essentially the same plan. In British East Africa, on the contrary, the Company, which had undertaken the administration of the country, abandoned the traditional British policy; it had no sooner occupied the coast towns than it advanced inland, and spent most of its energies and capital in a struggle for the remotest province in its territories, only concerning itself with the more easily ruled, intermediate country, in so far as it was necessary for the maintenance of communications with its garrison in Uganda.

Geographical explorers have followed the same system. The "back blocks" of British East Africa have been traversed in all directions and roughly surveyed, while there are areas a day's march from the coast, which, geographically, are quite unknown.

The necessity for the adventurous and expensive plunge into the heart of Africa, which ruined the British East African Company, can only be understood through a consideration of the physical structure of the country.

Geographically, British East Africa consists of seven belts of country, which run approximately parallel to the coast. The characters of each belt are strikingly unlike. The first belt consists of the coast plain and the off-lying islands; the second belt is the Nyika, a barren plateau stretching inland beyond the coast plain for a width of from seventy to two hundred miles; next come the volcanic plains of Masai-land, which lie between the Nyika and the eastern wall of the Erythrean or Great Rift Valley; then follows the fourth belt, the Great Rift Valley itself, bounded on the west by the scarp of the Mau-Kamasia plateau. This plateau, which forms the fifth belt, descends slowly to the sixth belt, the basin of the Victoria Nyanza. Lastly, we come to the Rift Valley of the Nile, the westernmost belt of British East Africa.

The first of these parallel belts with which the traveller becomes acquainted is that of the coastal plains; this belt, perhaps, appears the most interesting and promising district to a visitor from the temperate zone. The soil is rich, the rainfall, though irregular, is generally ample, and most of this belt, thanks to its damp, warm climate, could be tilled to a garden, growing all the fruits of the tropics, and supporting a dense population. The scenery, moreover, especially if seen from a dhow sailing along the coast, is pleasing and varied. Surf-beaten coral reefs occur at intervals along the shore, and behind the breakers is a shore passage, where boats lie in peace, safe from the heavy swell that rolls in from the Indian Ocean. Beyond the boat channel lies a beach of white, glistening, coral sand, backed here by yellow, palm-clad sandhills, and there by banks of soft blue mud, passing into green forests of mangrove and jungles of screw pines; while elsewhere, straight above the white broken waters of the reef belt, stand grey cliffs of raised coral rock, weathered into caves and crags, and capped by a bright red soil.

Beyond the cliffs, and along the valleys, there are palm groves, fruit orchards, rice fields, banana plantations, well-tilled fields of yams, maize, earth-nuts and beans; and, nestling in the hollows, are villages of oblong huts made of interlaced palm leaves or of wattle and daub. Between the cultivated areas are wide tracts of acacia scrub, and forests of branching palms, and of native teak, ebony, and other timber trees; these forests are generally rendered almost impenetrable by vines and creepers and thick tropical undergrowth.

Westward, the belt of the coast plain and the low coast hills ends at the foot of a steep slope, which looks like one side of a mountain range; but, on ascent, it proves to be the eastern scarp of the great East African plateau. This hill face is well seen from Mombasa, and the Uganda Railway climbs it immediately after reaching the mainland; but in other parts of the British sphere the coastal belt is wider, and the scarp is farther inland; while, where it has been breached by the rivers, there is a long gradual ascent into the interior by a valley, instead of by one steep, short climb.

From the edge of this slope a vast undulating plain extends, as far as the eye can follow it, into the interior. Most of the plain is a turfless, sandy waste, waterless except in the rainy season.

This desert belt, which is known as the Nyika, has generally left a very unpleasing impression on the minds of travellers who have marched across it at the end of the dry season. It is described by Mr. Scott-Elliot, who looked upon it with the interest of a botanical specialist, as "a most curious district. Gnarled and twisted acacias of all sorts and sizes, usually with bright, white bark and a very thin and naked appearance, cover the whole country. Amongst these one finds the flat-topped acacia, and curious trees of euphorbia. The grasses and sedges in this part grow in little tufts, at some distance from one another, leav-

THE BAOBAB TREE.

GEOGRAPHY OF BRITISH EAST AFRICA 9

ing the general tint of the landscape that of the soil itself. No sward or turf is formed, and, except immediately after the rains, all these grasses are dead, dry and withered up. Most of the plants are either thorny or fleshy, as is usual in all desert countries."[1]

At the end of the rainy season the Nyika may look green and fertile, but, as soon as the rains cease, the pitiless tropical sun scorches the vegetation, sucks up the rain pools, and turns the rush-bordered stream courses into sandy nullahs. For a while, a sheet of cabbage-like *Stratiotis* and the broad-leaved lotus protects the swamps, which remain as oases in the desert; but, under the hot blast from the surrounding plains, the leaves wither, and, thus uncovered, the water is soon evaporated by the envious sun; a layer of mud, soon as dry as a sun-baked brick, covers the floor of the water holes, and the oasis is merged in the dreary, desert waste.

This belt of Nyika extends right across British East Africa from north to south, broken only by the valleys of the Sabaki, Tana and Juba rivers. Along the Tana the soil is so rich and deep, that the forest belt beside the river is impenetrable, except where native paths or game tracks have bored a passage through the undergrowth.

Though the Nyika has been described as a plain, its

---

[1] G. F. Scott-Elliot, *A Naturalist in Mid-Africa*.

surface is by no means level, for the belt is composed of rocks of great antiquity, with bands of very unequal hardness. The action of stream, rain and wind-borne sand has cut so deeply into the Nyika, that its surface is always undulating, and it is at intervals broken by steep, hog's-back ridges and boulder-strewn hills. The highest of these hills are the remnants of the oldest mountain range in British East Africa; they occur as a series of ridges (mostly near the meridian of 38° E. long.), and they rise to the height of from 5,000 to 7,000 feet above the sea.

To the west of the Nyika are the broad lava plains of Kapti, the Athi and Laikipia. This belt is probably the most hopeful region in British East Africa, for the soil is fertile and the climate healthy; the days are often hot, but the nights are always cool, and Europeans can live and labour in this district with less discomfort and ill-health than in any other part of Equatorial Africa. When the grass of these plains is low in the dry season, the soft, short turf, the dome-shaped hills and the well-rounded, streamless valleys give the country the aspect of some of our English chalk downs; and, when timbered, the country is beautifully parklike. The volcanic belt, however, includes some rugged hill country, clad in dense forests, wherein are found the great food plantations of the Kikuyu. To this zone also belong the great volcanic piles of Kenya and Settima.

The lava plains are abruptly terminated by the Great Rift Valley, the most remarkable feature in the geography of Eastern Africa. This valley has been formed by the subsidence of the block of material that once filled it. At one time the surface of the volcanic plains to the east of the Rift Valley were continuous with the similar plains to the west. Parallel cracks, hundreds of miles in length, broke across the rocks; the block of material between these cracks sank, leaving walls, in places, so precipitous that the Uganda Railway has had temporarily to use a cable-worked funicular railway for the descent into the valley from the Kikuyu plateau. The walls of the valley, however, are not always precipitous. The lines along which the subsidence occurred cut across ridges, valleys and basins; and the character of the scarps that now bound the valley varies with the structure of the country on either side of the Rift Valley.

In British East Africa there are two main rift valleys. The eastern, known as the Erythrean, or Great Rift Valley, extends through East Africa from the German frontier to Abyssinia; it bends eastward round the Abyssinian plateau, and reaches the southern end of the Red Sea; it is then continued northward by the Red Sea and Gulf of Akaba to the valley, which leads over the Arabah depression to the Dead Sea and Jordan Valley.

Beyond the western wall of the Great Rift Valley the

country slopes gradually to the depression, the lowest part of which is occupied by the Victoria Nyanza. The floor of the Nyanza basin is fairly level, as a rule, but it is intersected by numberless broad, shallow, flat-floored valleys.

"The whole of Uganda, Usoga, and much of Karagwe," says Scott-Elliot, "consists of an infinity of hills and ridges 4,110 feet, on an average, above the sea. Their flat valleys are usually occupied by swamp rivers, often half a mile wide. These curve and twist about in an extraordinary fashion, and have numerous minor swamps connected with them. It is thus immediately obvious that railways are impossible, and roads extremely difficult. In a course of twenty miles we may have to cross eight swamps from a quarter to three-quarters of a mile wide, and mount and descend twelve hills each 300 feet high and also steep."

These swampy valleys are lined with rich, deep soil, and the country is at a lower level than most of the volcanic country to the east. Lake Naivasha, in the Rift Valley, is 6,230 feet above the sea, but the level of the Nyanza is only 3,820 feet. Hence Uganda and the countries around the Victoria Nyanza have a warmer climate, and are more typically tropical in their characters, than the high plateaux that separate them from the fertile coast lands.

West of the Nyanza basin is the second and western Rift Valley—that of the Nile. It lies between the high

GEOGRAPHY OF BRITISH EAST AFRICA 13

plateau of the Congo Free State to the west, and the snow-clad Ruwenzori and the plateau of Unyoro to the east. It is continued southward to Tanganyika, and northward down the valley of the Nile. Its formation was no doubt similar to that of the Erythrean Rift Valley, and Stanley's bold suggestion regarding the event has been justified by the evidence of later travellers. " Time was when Ruwenzori did not exist. It was grassy upland, extending from Unyoro to the Balegga plateau."[1] Then came the upheaval at a remote period. " Ruwenzori was raised to the clouds, and a yawning abyss 250 miles long and 30 miles broad lay south-west and north-east."

The Nilotic Rift Valley repeats the characters of the Erythrean Rift Valley, and it is occupied by long, narrow, fiord-like lakes, of a very different aspect from the round lakes, with low, shelving shores, of the Victoria Nyanza type.

The contrast between the two lake types is well expressed by the late Major Thruston :

"The ordinary conception of a lake under the Equator is of a sheet of water with swampy shores, infested by myriads of mosquitoes, surrounded by dense tropical forest, with rank undergrowth and a tangled mass of creepers. Such would be a fairly correct description of Lake Victoria. Lake Albert is very different. Its

---

[1] The country to the west of the Albert Nyanza.

eastern shore is bounded by a steep and sometimes precipitous bank from 1,000 to 1,500 feet in height, the edge of the water being fringed by a plain varying from a few feet to a mile in breadth. . . . The western shore is formed by a chain of lofty mountains, the highest peaks of which must be at least 8,000 feet above the level of the lake. The sides of the mountains are like walls rising out of the water. . . . The whole scene resembles a fiord in Norway."

Such, then, in broad outline, is the physical structure of British East Africa. It is a land of striking contrasts, both in climate and in geographical characters. Although lying across the Equator, there are two mountains, Kenya and Ruwenzori, that are always snow-capped, and the volcanic plateaux bear many plants whose affinities are with those of the Mediterranean basin. Again, the country exhibits the action of both ice and fire : it has a system of glaciers; it has also innumerable old volcanoes. These last occur both as weathered cones in the last stages of decay, and as lines of well-preserved craters, where the old volcanic fires are not yet wholly extinct. It is a land, moreover, of lakes and deserts. In the western basin is the second largest freshwater lake in the world, and in the Rift Valleys are fiord-like lakes, one of which, Lake Rudolf, is 170 miles in length ; while in contrast to these vast existing lakes there are barren tracts of

> "The shining plain that is said to be
> The dried-up bed of a tormer sea,
> Where the air, so dry, and so clear and bright,
> Reflects the sun with a wondrous light,
> And out in the dim horizon makes
> The deep blue gleam of the phantom lakes."

The essential fact, then, in the economic geography of British East Africa, is its remarkable diversity. It contains all sorts of climate and all varieties of soils; we find the fertile, fever-stricken belt of the coastlands; the broad, undulating, arid waste of the Nyika; the high, bracing, turf-clad plains of Masai-land; and the deep, wind-swept trough of the Great Rift Valley; as well as the warm, rich lowlands of the Nyanza basin and the valley of the Upper Nile, where palms flourish, and both vegetation and climate have a tropical character.

The temperate character of the plateau country renders it more suitable for European settlement than the low-lying zones on either side; but so long as the highlands remain sparsely inhabited, they will be of less commercial value than the more densely populated and richer country of Uganda. Hence the British East Africa Company was only adapting its policy to the natural conditions of the country when it devoted its best energies to the occupation of the well-populated lowlands of the interior, and to the establishment of a direct connection between them and the coast towns. The British Government has been forced to follow the same plan, and, at the cost of many millions, is building a railway from Mombasa to the Victoria Nyanza ; yet both British administrations are only following the example of the Arab traders, who were the pioneers in the economic development of Eastern Africa.

Chapter II

THE NATIVES OF BRITISH EAST AFRICA

> "But no! they rubb'd through yesterday
> In their hereditary way,
> And they will rub through, if they can,
> To-morrow on the selfsame plan,
> Till death arrive to supersede,
> For them, vicissitude and need."
>
> —*Matthew Arnold.*

SOME acquaintance with the races, as well as with the geography, of British East Africa is necessary for a correct understanding of the history of the country. The tribes that live there belong to several distinct race groups. Some deplorable incidents in the recent history of the protectorate would probably never have occurred had due allowance been made for the fundamental differences in character between members of the various races.

The population, in the main, consists of negroes. They belong to that section of the negro race known as the Bantu, which occupies most of Africa, south of a line from the Cameroons on the west coast to the mouth of the Juba on the east coast. The typical Bantu tribes of British East Africa are the Wa-nyika, with their allies the Wa-duruma and Wa-giriama, who inhabit the eastern part of the Nyika and the southern part of the coastal belt; the Wa-taita, who live in the Taita mountains in the south-western part of the Nyika, beginning some eighty-five miles west from Mombasa; the Wa-kamba, who occupy the hilly country in the basin of the River Athi, along the western boundary of the Nyika; and the Wa-pokomo, who dwell on the banks of the lower Tana, from the edge of the plateau country at Hameye to the sea.

The Bantu of British East Africa are, as a rule, peaceful and industrious agriculturists. The Wa-kamba are the bravest, the most enterprising, and the most intelligent; while the Wa-pokomo are probably the most industrious, as they are certainly the most timid, of the Bantu tribes.

The Bantu tribes are pagans, and have so far yielded unsatisfactory returns to missionary enterprise. Missions have been established for half a century among the Wa-nyika, with meagre results. The Scottish Industrial Mission to the Kikumbuliu section of the Wa-kamba has been removed, after a few years' work, to a more hopeful clan; but, according to Thruston, even the best of the Wa-kamba have decided that "they will have nothing to say to the Gospel, which they consider a most improbable story."

The Bantu section of the negro race is also represented by some hybrid tribes, formed by the intermarriage of foreign immigrants with the primitive Bantu stock. Of these mixed races the most important is that of the Suahili, whose language, Ki-suahili, is the *lingua franca* of East Africa. The Suahili live along the coast lands and in the islands of Pemba and Zanzibar. The name is derived from Suahil, a coast, and the race has been formed by the intermarriage of Arab, Persian and Beluchi traders, with the Bantu of the coast lands, or with members of the inland tribes, who have been taken to the coast as slaves. The better-class Suahili live in the eastern ports, and they conduct most of the trade with the interior. Many East Africans, who are called Arabs, are really Suahili. Frequent reference will be made in subsequent chapters to Arab traders and Arab caravans, but it must be understood that the name is used conventionally, and is not anthropologically correct. Tippu Tib is a typical Suahili; his mother was a Bantu slave, his father a half-caste Arab. But Tippu is usually called an Arab, in accordance with the East African use of the word, as the name of a caste, rather than of a race.

The Wa-ganda are another tribe with a Bantu basis altered and improved by intermixture with people who do not belong to the negro race. The primitive Bantu of Uganda were conquered by the Wa-huma, a Hamitic tribe allied to the Galla and to some of the Abyssinians. Some remnants of pure Wa-huma still survive in the Uganda Protectorate. That they are not negroes was recognised by the first travellers in Uganda. "The Wa-huma," says Stanley, "are true descendants of the Semitic [1] tribes or communities, which emigrated from Asia across the Red Sea, and settled on the coast, and in the uplands of Abyssinia, once known as Ethiopia."

It is to this foreign intermixture that the Wa-ganda owe their political importance and personal intelligence.

Another type of the negro race is represented by the Kikuyu, a tribe which lives in a belt of forest country extending from the southern slopes of Kenya to the edge of the Great Rift Valley. The Kikuyu differ from the Bantu in many respects, and appear to be allied to the Niamniam of the Congo Free State rather than to any other tribe in East Africa. They may be the offspring of intermarriage between the Bantu and the Nilotic races.

The Nilotic group is represented by the Masai, a race of pastoral, warlike nomads, who roam over the grazing plains of the volcanic belt and of the Rift Valley. They are allied to the negroes of the Nile Valley, and must have invaded British East Africa from the north and north-west. The Masai are brave and warlike, and the whole social organization of the tribe is adapted for

---

[1] This may have been a *lapsus calami* for Hamitic.

IVORY TRADERS IN MASAI DRESS.

Photo.—
Imperial British
E. Africa Co.

NATIVES OF BRITISH EAST AFRICA

the training of warriors, who undertake cattle-raiding expeditions against their neighbours.

The Masai had a wide reputation for ferocity, bloodthirstiness, and fickleness, and Kipling's "Some take their tucker with tigers, and some with the giddy Masai" illustrates the character they once enjoyed. Before British East Africa fell under British influence the Masai were a scourge to the whole country, and they prevented much of the best land from being cultivated. Of the Bantu tribes only the Wakamba could hold their own against the Masai; and even they had to leave untilled much of the best land in their country, for they could not protect exposed portions.

As late as 1889 the Masai raided in sight of Mombasa; they frequently quarrelled with Arab caravans, which they annihilated; they have killed several Europeans during the last few years, and in 1894 massacred a Government caravan of over 1,000 porters. Cattle disease, however, has now broken their power and reduced their numbers, and they are not likely to give serious trouble to the British Administration; but their military system and power to mass rendered them, at one time, more dangerous than any other tribe in British East Africa.

The Nilotic race is also represented among the people of Kavirondo, whose most striking characteristic is their absolute nudity. But, as is often the case in Africa, nudity is accompanied by morality; some of their fully-clad neighbours are far less moral than these naked natives of Kavirondo. Hobley's researches show that the Wa-kavirondo include a mixture of races, but the main basis of population appears to be the Nilotic negro. Another tribe of the same race are the Nyempsians, the best British East African representative of the peoples called Wakwafi; these tribes have been regarded as degenerate Masai, who had lost their cattle and taken to agricultural pursuits. But, according to evidence collected by New, the first Englishman to study them, these Wakwafi are a distinct race, who have been crushed and dispossessed by the Masai invasion. This view is the more probable.

The Hamitic race is represented in British East Africa by the Galla. One section of this tribe lives along the Tana Valley, and in the plains between that river and the Sabaki. Early in the nineteenth century the Galla were of greater importance than at present, and they ruled the country from the Juba to Mombasa. They then gained a great reputation for cruelty and ferocity. Boteler, who surveyed the eastern coast in 1822-1826, tells us that "the Gallah have no houses, but wander in the woods in the wildest state. Professed enemies to every native and tribe around them, they hunt and are hunted, committing indiscriminate slaughter on unresisting multitudes one day, and becoming the victims of like treatment from a superior force of their enemies on the next.'

NATIVES OF BRITISH EAST AFRICA 23

But at present the power of the Galla is insignificant, and this interesting tribe, including the most intellectual of the East African natives, is of little political importance. Their allies, the Randile, living in the country east of Lake Rudolf, are, however, still numerous and prosperous, having great herds of camels and cattle.

The last element in the population of British East Africa is a survival of the aboriginal pygmy. This race is represented on the western edge of the country by true pure-bred pygmies, who have been studied by Stühlmann. To the east of the Rift Valley there is a dwarf tribe of historic interest, as it supplied the first modern confirmation of the classical and mediæval reports of the existence of pygmies in Central Africa. This tribe, however, has been much altered by negro intermixture, so that its members are only half-castes. The tribe was first reported from Abyssinia under the name of the Doko. The earliest detailed account of them was published by Sir. W. C. Harris, but it was apparently written by Krapf.[1] Subsequently rumours of the existence of a

[1] In *The Great Rift Valley*, p. 327, I regret to have done an injustice to Krapf, by accusing him of plagiarism from Harris. The two men published a detailed account of the Doko in practically identical language. Harris's account appeared in 1844 and Krapf's in 1860. I therefore concluded that Krapf had copied from Harris; but Krapf elsewhere declares that, while in Abyssinia, he lent his note books to Harris, who published long extracts from them without acknowledgment. Krapf felt at liberty to reprint his notes, without reference to their prior publication by Harris;

southern section of the tribe, mentioned as the Waberikimo, were reported from Mombasa by Boteler and Rigby. Members of the northern tribe, or Doko, have been seen by Dr. Donaldson Smith, while the southern tribe has been described by the author.

he thereby laid himself open to a charge of plagiarism, which I gladly now withdraw.

BOOK II

THE GEOGRAPHICAL PIONEERS

"We were dreamers, dreaming greatly, in the man-stifled town;
We yearned beyond the sky-line, where the strange roads go down."

—*Kipling*.

Chapter III

THE DAWN OF EAST AFRICAN GEOGRAPHY

> "Far hence, upon the Mountains of the Moon,
> Is my abode; where heaven and nature smile,
> And strew with flowers the secret bed of Nile."
> —*Dryden.*

THE modern period in the geography of Equatorial Africa began with Bruce's *Travels in Abyssinia*, and the foundation of the African Association,—the parent of the Royal Geographical Society. But long before the time of Bruce and Park, Eastern Africa had been explored and exploited by trávellers, who had discovered most of the leading facts in the geography of Equatorial Africa. As is shown by Sanson d'Abbeville's map of Equatorial Africa published in 1635, it was known early in the seventeenth century that the Congo rose from Lake Zaire or Tanganyika, and that the Nile sprang from a series of lakes. Indeed, the outline of " Zaflan Lacus," the largest of these lakes, is more correctly represented in Sanson's map of 1635 than it is in the map of Africa in the latest edition of the *Encyclopædia Britannica*. The early geographers knew, moreover, of the existence of Lake Rudolf, which was not seen by any European until 1889; and they marked the courses of the two chief rivers of British East Africa, the Tana and Sabaki, with greater accuracy than was done in our maps of ten years ago.

In fact, the end of the first half of the nineteenth century is the period when European ignorance of the geography of Central Africa reached its climax; the reports of early travellers had been dismissed as lies and fables, and the whole interior of the continent was represented as an uninhabited, desert waste.

But these early explorations must not be forgotten, as the reports to which they gave rise, inspired interest in Central Africa, and guided later travellers to their goal.

At what date the exploration of the interior of East Africa began is unknown, for some of the results are quoted in the oldest known literature. On early Egyptian monuments there are figures of the equatorial dwarfs, with the name "Akka" written beside them. These drawings show that at the time when they were made there was intercourse between Egypt and the highlands on the south-western part of the Nile basin. The first pages of existing literature show some knowledge of Equatorial Africa. Homer states that when, to escape the northern winter,—

> "To warmer seas the cranes embodied fly,
> With noise and order, thro' the mid-way sky,
> To pygmy nations wounds and death they bring."

As the flamingoes of the Mediterranean migrate every winter to the Upper Nile, where the pygmies still live, this passage shows that, even in Homer's time, the Greeks knew something of the more striking marvels of Eastern Equatorial Africa.

The indications of this knowledge become more precise in the works of later classical authors, and, before the beginning of the Christian Era, the Greek geographers certainly possessed much reliable information about Equatorial Africa.

This knowledge was no doubt obtained, in the first instance, from traders, some of whom journeyed south, across the Sahara or up the Nile, while others sailed down the Red Sea into the Indian Ocean, and along the East African coast.

The trade was probably begun and developed by the Phœnicians, for Solomon's joint enterprise with Hiram of Tyre is the first recorded commercial venture in Eastern Africa. The ships were built on the Red Sea at Eziongeber in the land of Edom. Hiram supplied the seamen and Solomon the commercial travellers. Once every three years the fleet returned from Ophir, with "gold and silver, ivory, and apes and peacocks."

If the peacocks were guinea-fowl, as has been not unreasonably suggested, then Solomon's Ophir may well have been in South-Eastern Africa. That Phœnician or Sabean influence reached the Zambesi is shown by the famous ruin of Zimbabwe in Mashona-land. It is probable that this temple was built by the traders, who worked the goldfields of British South Africa centuries before the Christian era.

We are not, however, compelled to rely on any doubtful identification, such as the site of Solomon's Ophir must always remain. The writings of classical geographers contain definite evidence of the early exploration of Equatorial Africa. Herodotus tells us of the journey of some young men from Nassamonia, a country to the west of Lower Egypt, who crossed the Sahara to a river, which is generally believed to be the Niger. He further records the circumnavigation of Africa, two centuries before his time, by some mariners sent out by Pharaoh Necho. These men were Phœnicians, who entered the Egyptian service; ships were built on the Red Sea, and the expedition started southward. It passed through the Straits of Bab-el-Mandeb, out into the Indian Ocean, and slowly made its way down the East African coast. Several times the stores of food were exhausted, and the mariners had to haul their boats ashore, and sow a crop of grain. They waited until it had grown, and when it was harvested, the boats were launched again on the arduous voyage. At length the explorers reached the southern coast of what is now Cape Colony; they steered westward, with the sun on their right hand, until they again turned to the north, entered the Mediterranean through the Pillars of Hercules, and reached Egypt after an absence of three years.

Herodotus, himself, dismisses the report as fabulous, owing to the assertion that, during part of the voyage, the sun was on their right hand. This statement, however, is now regarded as probably the strongest evidence in favour of the truth of the narrative.

The objects of Solomon's southern venture were avowedly commercial, and the first Egyptian expeditions were probably inspired by the same motive. But the Egyptian traders were soon followed by geographers anxious to solve the problem, why the Nile should rise in flood during the hottest and driest season of the year. The explanation, that it was due to snow on high mountains melting in the summer, had even then been suggested; for Herodotus argues against the theory on the ground of the high temperature of the country south of Egypt, as proved by the heat of the south wind, the blackness of the natives, and the southward flight of the cranes to avoid the winter cold. The snow theory being dismissed as improbable, the behaviour of the Nile remained a puzzle which specially roused the interest of the speculative Greeks. Thus the first question that Alexander the Great put to the oracle of Jupiter Ammon was an inquiry respecting the sources of the Nile. Nero sent an army up the Nile to trace the river to its head, while the wiser Ptolemy Philadelphus endeavoured to solve the problem by sending an expedition overland from the eastern coast. That the origin of the Nile was a source of interest to the Romans in the time of Nero may be seen in the *Pharsalia*, where Lucan makes Cæsar say that he would abandon the career of arms, if he could see the Nile fountains.

That the repeated efforts to reach the Upper Nile were rewarded by definite information about the source of that river, is proved by the works of the classical geographers. They show that the Nile rises from three lakes in the equatorial regions, and that, later on, it is joined by the Blue Nile from Abyssinia. This knowledge is evident in Hipparchus' map, and the same information is repeated, with much additional matter, in Ptolemy's map and writings, A.D. 150.

Before Ptolemy, however, an account of the East African coast was issued in an Egyptian "Pilot's Guide to the Indian Ocean," which was compiled towards the end of the first century A.D.

This work[1] is of interest, as it gives the earliest description of Zanzibar. The name of the author is unknown. The title of the book is the "Periplus of the Red Sea" (*Periplus Maris Erythraei*). Its authorship was once referred to Arrian.

The exact date of the work is uncertain, but that it is earlier than the time of Ptolemy is evident from its

[1] A text in Greek and Latin, with elaborate notes, is published in Müller's Lesser Greek Geographers (1855), vol. i. pp. 257-305.

DAWN OF EAST AFRICAN GEOGRAPHY 33

less accurate information regarding India. The author's information was probably obtained from the logs of the mariners and traders, who had journeyed into the Indian Ocean. The *Periplus* describes the sailing route down the Red Sea, and round Cape Aromata (Cape Guardafui). The country near it was rich in frankincense, myrrh, and spices. After passing the Cape, the route lay along the East African coast, and during the voyage the merchants exchanged corn, wine and weapons for ivory, tortoiseshell and rhinoceros horns.

A translation of the description of the East African coast in the *Periplus*, for which I am indebted to my colleague, Professor Tucker, is given in an appendix to this chapter (page 49).

Ptolemy's account is more detailed. The passages are worth quoting as the first description of East Africa, of which we know the date and author. The translation is by Dr. Schlichter.

" Going from Arabia to Aromata, the course passes the country of Barbaria; after Aromata, there is a bay, and the village of Panum situated in it, one day's journey distant from Aromata. From this village the emporium of Opone is distant another day's journey, and then comes a second bay. Here begins the country of Azania, near the promontory of Zingis, and the mountain of Phalangis, which has three peaks. This bay is called Apocopa, and can be passed in two days and two nights. Then, three courses distant, we find the

Little Strand, and another place which is called the Great Strand, and is five courses distant from the former; both these distances can be accomplished by sailing in four days and four nights. Then follows another bay, in which is situated an emporium called Essina, reached after a further navigation of one day and one night; and then commences the bay, which extends to Rhapta and is a three days' and three nights' journey by ship. Near the beginning of this bay is an emporium, which is called Tonike, and not far from the promontory of Rhaptum is the river Rhaptus, and the capital with the same name, the latter being inland, but not far from the coast. From Rhaptum to the promontory of Praesum extends a very large but shallow bay, the shores of which are inhabited by cannibals."

In a later passage Ptolemy continues:

"Ethiopia, which is situated south of these regions, and of the whole country of Libya, is terminated northward by a line, reaching from the promontory of Rhaptum to the large bay of the exterior ocean, and by that part of the western ocean which is near it. West and south it is terminated by unknown country. On the eastern side it reaches from the promontory of Rhaptum and bay of Barbaria (which is called the 'rough sea,' on account of the force of the waves) to the promontory of Praesum. After that the country is unknown."

Still more important than Ptolemy's knowledge of

the coast line is the fact that he had some acquaintance with the ivory-yielding hinterland. For he tells us that to the west of his cannibal-haunted bay, between Praesum and Rhaptum, extend the mountains of the Moon, from which the Nile lakes receive the snows. It is true that the positions assigned by Ptolemy to these lakes were inaccurate, but this mistake was inevitable, as he had to rely only on the recollections of rough-route traverses by native traders. Cooley dismissed Ptolemy's information as the result of a few lucky guesses. But the closeness of the coincidence, and the fact that Ptolemy was a scientific geographer and not a guesser, render this view improbable. The information is sufficiently accurate, in the essential points, to show that the east-coast caravans must, even at this early date, have worked their way to the high plateau of the interior.

Ptolemy's belief that the Nile was fed by melting snow is interesting, as it shows that all the classical authorities were not convinced by Herodotus' arguments. But for the first certain evidence of the existence of snow-capped mountains in Eastern Africa we have to turn to the Arabian geographers, who, after the fall of the Mediterranean school, continued the exploitation of the country.

The Arabians and Persians had probably conducted an East African ivory and slave trade from the remotest antiquity. Many of the Persian tales are based on the adventures of their sailors on the eastern coast. Sinbad the Sailor's powerful bird, the roc, for instance, is most likely the now extinct Æpyornis of Madagascar, which laid truly colossal eggs; and Reinaud, it may be remembered, has identified the Isles of Wak-Wak as the Zanzibar group.

After the Mohammedan conquest of Egypt, the Arabian geographers became as interested in the mystery of the Nile as the Greeks had been, and they explored the Nile Valley as well as the eastern coast. Stanley quotes Abdul Hassan Ali, an Arab geographer, who was born at Bagdad and settled in Egypt in A.D. 955, as saying :

"I have seen, in a geography, a plan of the Nile flowing from the Mountains of the Moon—Jebel Kumr. The waters burst forth into twelve springs and flow into two lakes, like unto the ponds of Bussora. After leaving these lakes the waters reunite, and flow through a sandy and mountainous country. The course of the Nile is through that part of the Soudan near the country of the Zenj (Zanzibar)."

Hence the Arabs believed in the "Mountains of the Moon" as firmly as did Ptolemy. Edrisi, a twelfth-century geographer, also tells us that the Nile rises from two lakes, which discharge their water into a third; this is exactly true of the Nile, and he adds that these lakes are all to the north of the "Mountains of the Moon."

DAWN OF EAST AFRICAN GEOGRAPHY

Two centuries later (in 1331) the famous Arab explorer, Sheikh Ibn Batuta, during the course of his 75,000 miles of wandering, visited the east coast and described Mombasa. He calls it a large town, and speaks of the natives as "chaste, honest and religious," but he tells us nothing of the interior, and it is not until the seventeenth century that we get the first definite account of the East African snow fields.

An Arab manuscript, of the year of the Hegira 1098 (A.D. 1686), which Stanley gives in a translation, discusses the old problem of the periodic floods of the Nile:

"Some say that its rise is caused by snow melted in summer, and, according to the quantity of snowfall, will be the greater or lesser rise." "The Nile," it continues, "starts from the Mountains of Gumr beyond the Equator. There is a difference of opinion as to the derivation of the word 'Gumr.' Some say it ought to be pronounced 'Kamar,' which means the sun; but the traveller, Ti Tarshi, says that it was called by that name because 'the eye is dazzled by the great brightness.' Some say that people have ascended the mountain, and one of them began to laugh and clap his hands, and threw himself down on the further side of the mountain. The others were afraid of being seized with the same fit, and so came back. It was said that those who saw it saw bright snows, like white silver, glistening with light."

Ibn Batuta's visit to Mombasa was in 1331, and his account shows that the Arabs were then in undisputed control of the coast lands; but, at the end of the next century, the Portuguese arrived upon the scene.

The first Portuguese expedition to visit East Africa was that of Vasco da Gama, who rounded the Cape of Good Hope, and, in 1498, worked his way northward to Melindi, whence he sailed across the ocean to India.

The various accounts of his expedition, though they differ in important particulars, give us a good idea of the state of the country at that time. The coast towns were all under Arab rule, and were far more flourishing than they have been in recent times.

Kilwa was a great rendezvous of the Arab traders, for Vasco da Gama's pilot told him "that Quilva was indeed a great city, and traded in much merchandise, which came from abroad in a great many ships from all parts, especially from Mekkah; and that, in the city, there were many kinds of people; and there were some Armenian traders, who were from a country called Armenia, and it was said that these people were Christians."

Vasco da Gama arrived at Mombasa on 7th April, 1498. He describes it as "a great city of trade, with many ships." The king sent the explorers "a large boat laden with fowls, sheep, sugar canes, citrons, lemons, and large, sweet oranges, the best that had ever been seen"; he also sent "a respectable old Moor" to welcome Da Gama, and to say that "his pleasure would be complete when the ships were at anchor within his port, if he could go in person to visit him on board of his ship"; and he hoped "that peace would last for ever between him and their king."

The old Moor returned with two of the Portuguese, one of whom was Peter Diaz. They were promised that 'they should have, without money, all that they saw and required, or that they asked for." They were taken to the houses of some Moors, "who feigned to be Christians, and who showed them beads with crosses, which they kissed and put in their eyes, and did great honour to our people for being Christians, making them sit down and eat cakes of rice, with butter and honey, and plenty of fruit."

Unfortunately, what appears to have been a misunderstanding broke off these friendly relations, and deprived us of any detailed account of Mombasa in the year 1498. The entrance to Mombasa Harbour is obstructed by coral reefs, and its navigation is often difficult. While working through the channel, Vasco da Gama's ship "missed stays," and began to drift towards the bank. The anchors were dropped, sails struck, and the danger averted. These proceedings were accompanied by much rushing and shouting on the part of the Portuguese crew; the native pilots, according to one account, were so terrified that some of them sprang overboard. Thereupon, Vasco da Gama suspected treachery; he seized the last of the pilots, and, by applications of boiling grease, made the poor wretch confess that the pilots had been ordered to wreck the ships. ,Vasco da Gama, accordingly, at once sailed northward. As Peter Diaz, one of the sailors who was ashore at the time of the mishap, was kindly treated by the natives, and at the first opportunity sent to India after Da Gama, the Portuguese suspicions were probably unfounded.

At Melindi, the next important port north of Mombasa, Vasco da Gama made a long stay, which enabled him to give a detailed account of that town. This description is worth notice, as showing the wealth and civilization which the country then enjoyed, and the simple friendliness with which the natives were prepared to welcome the new comers. In Vasco da Gama's description of Melindi, he tells us that "the city was a great one, of noble buildings, and surrounded by walls, and, placed immediately on the shore, it made an imposing appearance." The "king" invited the Portuguese ashore, and promised them every hospitality. But, remembering Mombasa, the suspicious da Gama declined the invitation, on the ground that "he and his men had been forbidden by their sovereign to land in foreign countries." As Camoens puts it—da Gama

"obeys his king's command,
That, till his orient mission be complete,
Nor coast nor harbour tempt him from the fleet.

DAWN OF EAST AFRICAN GEOGRAPHY 41

This excuse was accepted by the king, who forthwith made the expedition a generous present of food. He sent them a boat " laden with large copper kettles, and cauldrons of boiled rice, and very fat sheep roasted whole, and boiled, and much good butter, and thin cakes of wheat and rice flour, and many fowls, boiled and roast, stuffed with rice inside; also much vegetables and figs, cocoanuts, and sugar canes; and all in such quantities, that all the crews of the ships were sated." The Portuguese were soon convinced of the natives' sincerity, and landed in the town. The king looked after his visitors with oriental hospitality. " In order that our people should not be cheated in the price of things, the king ordered it to be cried all over the city, that nobody was to sell anything to the Portuguese for more than it was worth, and that if any one did so, he would send and burn his house, so that all observed this order." To mark his gratitude for the help given him in the refitting of his ships for the voyage to India, Vasco da Gama erected a pillar on an adjacent headland, and he told the king that he had been ordered not to do so "except in a country in which they knew true friendship and sincere love, such as you, sire, have shown us out of the greatness of your goodness."

The friendly relations between the Portuguese and the East African Arabs did not, however, long continue. Mvita, the native name for Mombasa, means " battle," and for some time after the arrival of the Portuguese, the name was only too well deserved.

After Vasco da Gama's return to Lisbon, a fleet was sent to India to annex and proselytize the country. Its commander, Cabral, was ordered to begin with preaching, and if that failed, to proceed to "the sharp determination of the sword." In 1500 he looted Mombasa, to avenge the supposed treachery to da Gama. In 1503 the town was again visited by a Portuguese fleet, and compelled to pay tribute. In August, 1505, it was attacked and destroyed by Francisco Almeyda with a fleet of twenty ships. Three years later the island was formally annexed to Portugal. But the inhabitants were turbulent, and gave so much trouble that in 1528 Don Zuna da Cunha was sent to raze the city to the ground, and it was captured after a desperate defence of four months. Later on the city was rebuilt, and its history was comparatively uneventful until 1586, when a Turkish fleet, under Ali Bey, visited Mombasa, which promptly placed itself under the suzerainty of the Porte.

A fleet from India, under Alfonso de Melo Bombeyro, punished this act of rebellion and defiance by again burning the town. Mombasa was soon rebuilt, but only to be burnt again—this time by a tribe of southern cannibals known as the Zimba, whose name is still current in the legends of the Suahili. The Zimba were soon expelled by the Portuguese, who, to secure their hold on the island, built the fort of Mombasa in 1594; the stone for the building is said to have been brought ready trimmed from Portugal.

The struggle between the Portuguese and the Arabs continued. In 1630 a revolt broke out under an apostate mission boy, Yusuf bin Ahmed, who attacked the fort. The Portuguese capitulated on condition that their lives should be spared, but the treacherous natives shot all their prisoners with arrows. A powerful force from India landed in Mombasa to avenge the massacre. Yusuf defended the fortress for three months, then dismantled it, and fled to Arabia in a captured Portuguese ship. In 1635 Xerxas de Cabreira rebuilt the fort, which still stands, and is the most picturesque and interesting building in British East Africa.

Until 1660 the Portuguese supremacy was undisputed, but then the Mazrui, the leading Arab clan on the east coast, entered into alliance with the Sultan of Muscat. This potentate is more correctly known as the Iman of Oman, the south-eastern province of Arabia. The allied Arab forces captured the fort of Mombasa after a five years' struggle, but the Portuguese still maintained their hold over the town and over part of the island; but in 1698 the Arabs were finally victorious, and the Portuguese for the last time were expelled from Mombasa.

The Portuguese, during their occupation of Mombasa, held it rather as a point of departure for India than for the sake of the country itself. They seemed to take small interest in the interior, and we learn little about it from them. Fernandez de Enciso, in his *Suma de Geographia* (1530), states that "West of this port [Mombasa] stands the Mount Olympus of Ethiopia, which is exceedingly high, and beyond it are the 'Mountains of the Moon,' in which are the sources of the Nile." His Mount Olympus, west of Mombasa, is probably Kilima Njaro.

De Barros, in 1552, records that the Arabs knew the Quilimanse[1] for thirty days' journey into the interior, and that negro caravans came to the coast, from the interior, with gold.

Much of the Portuguese information regarding the interior was doubtless derived from the Arabs, but that some of the Portuguese themselves went inland is known from various records: thus Marmol (1667) reports that a Portuguese named Fonseco explored the Quilimanse for five days' journey into the interior. It was probably the Portuguese who supplied the information in John Senex's map of 1711, which represents Baringo as an isolated lake without an outlet, although the contrary was incorrectly maintained by Livingstone and Burton, two and a half centuries later.

That Portuguese missionaries worked their way in-

[1] The name Quilimanse has been given to the Sabaki, Tana and Juba. In this case it is probably intended for the Sabaki, as the mouth of the river is said to be at Melindi.

DAWN OF EAST AFRICAN GEOGRAPHY 45

land is also probable from Sanson d'Abbeville's map. Opposite the head of the Tana and the northernmost tributary of the Sabaki, *i.e.* the Athi, is an isolated mountain, corresponding in position to Kenya. Against it is written, " N. D. Monasterium," which suggests that the Portuguese had a mission station in that district, as they certainly had in some of the other localities thus marked on the map.

In Equatorial Africa, however, the Portuguese made no such extensive explorations inland as they did further south in the Zambesi basin. The first detailed accounts of journeys in the interior we owe to the Arabs, who succeeded to supreme power on the coast after the expulsion of the Portuguese. To Arab traders belongs the honour of having first explored the interior of British East Africa, which they traversed in every direction. Most of the results of their work have, however, been lost, as there are no written records; but a number of itineraries were collected by Denhardt and published by him in 1881. In these itineraries Denhardt constructed a map which marks nearly every important lake, mountain, and river in British East Africa. The outlines are crude, and the relative positions often incorrect, but this map of 1881 was much fuller of detail than maps published some years later by European travellers. The journeys of these brave Arab and Suahili traders must be counted among the most remarkable feats of travel in the history of British East Africa, and their names are worthy of an honoured place in the roll of East African explorers.

Long before any European explorer had reached Naivasha or Baringo these lakes were marked on Denhardt's map, on the faith of the journey of Kamtima of Tanga. This trader started inland from Freretown, the Church Mission Settlement opposite Mombasa. He marched across the Nyika to Lake Jipe, at the south-eastern foot of Kilima Njaro; thence he struck northward past Taveta, round the western flank of Kilima Njaro, and over the Kapte Plains to Ngongo Bagas, the famous trading rendezvous at the south-western end of the Kikuyu country. Thence he marched along the Rift Valley to Lake Naivasha, and again on to the salt lake of Nakuro and the river Njoki (Nyuki), which flows through Njemps into Baringo. From Njemps, Kamtima continued along the Rift Valley, for two marches, to Kamasia, and thence to the country of the Suk. Three days more took him to a lake which Denhardt records as Baringo, but which must be Lake Rudolf, as the true Baringo is only six miles, and not six marches, from Njemps.

Further information regarding the Rift Valley, in the Naivasha to Baringo district, was obtained by Kaptao of Mombasa, who reported the existence of Doenyo Ngai, a still active steam vent in Masai-land, and who successfully crossed the dangerous country of Sotik.

Kaptao knew Lake Baringo, and of the existence to the south of it of the now well-known hot springs of Suva ya Moto, and the adjacent lake (Lake Losuguta), with "hot, bitter, stinking waters." The truth of Kaptao's report the present author found to his cost when he reached that lake waterless in 1893.

Another famous Arab traveller was Ferhaji of Pangani, who crossed the Mau plateau from Naivasha to the shores of the Victoria Nyanza in Kavirondo; thence he returned to Lake Baringo by a march which gives the first information about the now famous locality of Eldoma, the ravine by which the Uganda road leaves the Rift Valley. He refers to the locality as Eldomiano. Ferhaji was quite clear as to the distinction between the three lakes, the Victoria Nyanza, Baringo, and Lake Rudolf. The first he calls, apparently from its size, the Bahari dja Pili, "the Second Sea"; the name Baringo, he says, comes from Bahari Ndogo, "or Little Lake," while Lake Rudolf he refers to as Samburu. Ferhaji had reached Lake Rudolf from Naivasha, across the western margin of Laikipia, through the bamboo forests of Miansini, over the grazing plain of Rangatan Busi (Angata Wus as Denhardt spells it), round the northern flanks of Settima, and over the wooded ranges of Subugo, of most of which places we first hear in the narrative of this enterprising Suahili.

Another remarkable journey of Ferhaji's was from

Mombasa past Kilima Njaro to Naivasha, and thence across Laikipia to Ndoro at the western foot of Kenya. He skirted the Kenya forest belt to the north, and crossed the Djombeni Mountains, a range of which we first hear from European travellers, after the expedition of Chanler and von Höhnel in 1893. Ferhaji, in the same journey, also reached the vast swamp of Lake Lorian.

The Kenya district was visited by Mkaba of Ikanga, who made the first recorded traverse of Laikipia, from the foot of Kenya to Baringo.

Another route to Lake Rudolf, by the eastern foot of Kenya, was followed by Kamtjimi of Wasin. This intelligent trader brought back with him some remarkable information about a tribe of natives who live on a high mountain on the eastern shore of Lake Rudolf; these natives are said to be "Ristiani," and to "hold their goods in common, and believe in Issa and Mariam; and are therefore no heathens." They trade with the Somali and Abyssinians.

No travellers have yet found any Christians in this district, or any record of faith in Jesus or Mary, but the persistent native rumours of the existence of such a tribe, in the district east of Lake Rudolf, render it probable that there is a clan in that district which has retained some relics of the Christian faith, gained by their ancestors from Abyssinia, or from the missions of the Portuguese.

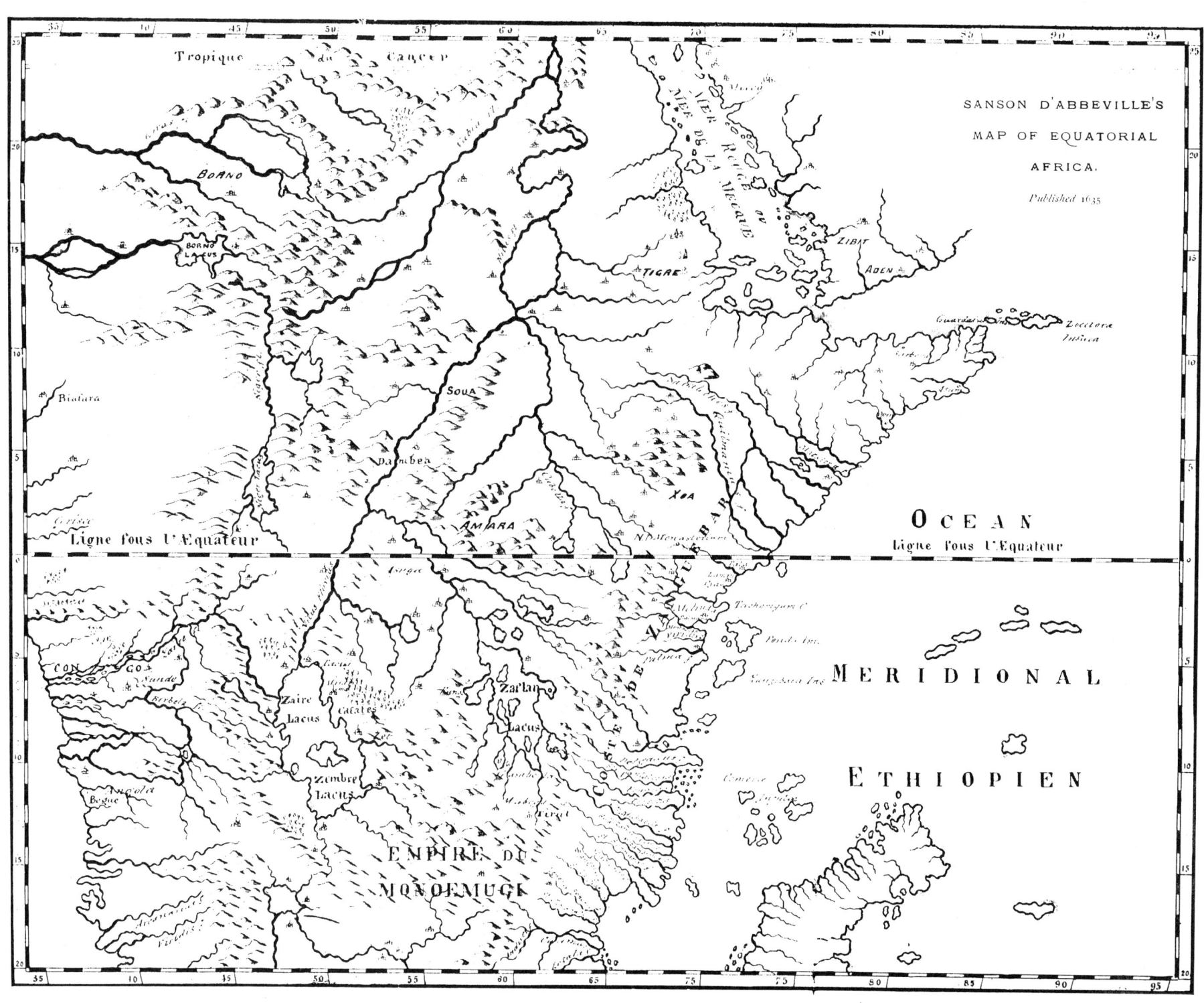

Appendix

ACCOUNT OF THE EAST AFRICAN COAST IN "THE PERIPLUS OF THE RED SEA," TRANSLATED BY PROFESSOR TUCKER

"From Opone [i.e. Afun or Hafun] the shore drawing more to the south,[1] first there come what are called the Little and Big Sheer-crests of Azania [2][by means of places for casting anchor, rivers] to the extent of six runs, the course being now due S.W. Then came the Little Beach and the Big Beach for another six runs, and next (there follow) in succession the runs[3] of Azania; in the first place, that which bears the name of Sarapion, then that of Nicon, following which are a number of rivers and other anchorages one after another, at intervals of stages and runs, to the number of seven altogether, as far as the Pyralaoi islands and what is called the Channel, from which, a little up from the S.W.,[4]

---

[1] i.e. the shore *first* runs S., and then, when the Apocopa begin, it runs exactly S.W. This I gather from the Greek, not the Atlas.

[2] Text corrupt. (I suppose he said that there were spots where you could cast anchor.)

[3] The language denotes that the name was established and recognised for that part.

[4] i.e. "*back* up" from S.W. and more towards E. So, at least, I should understand it if I had no maps and no knowledge of the place referred to.

after two runs of a day and night * * * (running)[1] exactly westerly[2] there meets you the island [3] Menuthias,[4]

[1] Text meaningless.

[2] The name slightly corrupted.

[3] *i.e.* the island, as you meet it in coming to it, stretches to W. But the text immediately following is a jargon, and there is no deciding precisely to what παρ' αὐτὴν τὴν δύσυν refers.

[4] If by this island he meant Zanzibar, it is most remarkable that he did not mention Pemba. His ποταμοὶ is applicable to a "stream" of any size, and need not be taken as much argument. (I don't know whether there are "streams" in Pemba.) On the other hand, his next section carries us past Zanzibar, and ignores it if *this* island is Pemba; and surely he would mention Zanzibar. I feel that there is no sort of certainty as to the amount of accidental omission from our text. The letters ειτενηδιωμ may be all that remains of something (beginning with ἐκτείνει or the like) which dropped out because followed by a similar-looking clause beginning with εἶτα or the like. It is useless to guess. On the whole, I feel convinced that he has lumped Pemba and Zanzibar together— to this extent, that the island which "meets" you "a little way back from S.W." is Pemba, but the general description is of Zanzibar. In other words, if you come your "two runs of a day and a night" from "the Channel," you will be "met," a "little more E. of your S.W. course," by an island which presents you with a coast "running west." This ought to be the N. coast of Pemba. Now, assuming that this N. coast of Pemba was familiar by sight to our sailor friends, they probably knew little more about the island, although, again, they did know something more of Zanzibar. In any case our author appears to me to have got already a little out of his own distance, and to be, as I say, lumping information.

Nevertheless, the gap may be considerable in the corrupt portion, and he may have spoken of Pemba first and Zanzibar next. Omissions of the sort are not rare in Greek MSS.

about 300 stades [37 miles] from the land, low-lying and covered with trees, in which are rivers, and very many sorts of birds, and tortoises. Of wild animals, it contains none at all except crocodiles,[1] but they hurt no man. There are in it little boats sewn together, or made of a single log, which they use for fishing and catching turtle. In this island they also snare them in a peculiar manner with baskets, which they let down instead of nets about the openings [inlets] of the foreshore."

[1] We have no right to suppose that the author thought them to be anything else, whatever they may have been in reality.

Chapter IV

THE MOMBASA MISSIONS

" He hath showed His people the power of His works, that He may give them the heritage of the heathen."

THE geographical reports of the early Portuguese and Arab traders were unconvincing and inadequate. They were the work of men who kept no journals, who took no observations, and who, on their return, could only tell rough yarns, like those on which Defoe founded his story of Captain Singleton's adventures in Madagascar and march across Africa. The critical geographers of the early part of the present century, accordingly, dismissed all the available evidence as mere travellers' tales, unworthy of notice outside of a nursery. Hence, while maps of the seventeenth and eighteenth centuries were full of details regarding the interior of Africa, the maps of the continent, between 1820 and 1850, represented the whole interior as an unknown, unvisited blank.

The tales of the Arab traders, however, roused the curiosity of more skilled explorers, and thus led to the next stage in the exploration of the interior, the work

THE MOMBASA MISSIONS 53

of the geographical pioneers. The pioneers in the exploration of Eastern Equatorial Africa were Dr. Ludwig Krapf and Sir Richard Burton, who were sent to the East African coast on missions at a time when Europe had little concern or interest in that region. Both men fell under the spell of its singular and powerful fascination.

Burton, with his usual facility in acquiring languages and winning the confidence of Orientals, gained the intimacy of the men who led caravans into the interior, and of slaves who remembered the land of their birth. The natives told him of great lakes, one of them so vast and stormy that they called it the "Second Sea." These tales roused Burton's interest, and he resolved to explore the mysterious region around these inland seas.

Krapf was a man of quite another type of mind. He was a simple-hearted, pure-souled evangelist, who had settled on the eastern coast near Mombasa, in the service of the Church Missionary Society. His interests were religious, not scientific. At first he cared nothing about geographical exploration, except as the instrument by which the Gospel could be carried to the people of the interior. He studied the character of the natives in order to discover how to win their souls, and he compiled dictionaries and grammars of their languages that the people might learn the teachings of Christ.

The work of Krapf and Burton lay on the coast lands, but they both looked eagerly westward at the wall of the East African plateau, and longed to climb it. Krapf prayed daily that he might scale that "rampart of East African heathendom," and Burton made up his mind that he would follow the strange roads that led across it into the darkness of the unknown land beyond.

Burton was the more successful in rousing English interest in the interior of the country, for Krapf's reports were discredited as those of an untrained, unreliable missionary. But to Krapf is due the honour of beginning European exploration in Eastern Equatorial Africa.

Ludwig Krapf was born on the 11th January, 1810, and was the son of a Wurtemberg farmer. As he tells us in quaint narrative: "My father, whose circumstances were easy, followed farming, and lived in the village of Derendingen, near Tübingen." He was educated at Tübingen, where he showed great zeal as a student. He suffered severely during his passage through a period of philosophic doubt. When his mental struggle was over, he resolved to devote his life to the African mission service. He was trained for the work at a college in Basel, and then sent by the Church Missionary Society to Shoa, a province on the south-western border of Abyssinia. He was well received by the King of Shoa, and laboured there for some years; then he went back to Europe for a visit, and married

DR. LUDWIG KRAPF.

THE MOMBASA MISSIONS   55

during his stay there. On his return to Africa, in 1842, he found that Shoa had been closed to Protestant missionaries, a proceeding which he attributed to the intrigues of a French mission.

Krapf had taken especial interest in the tribe of Galla who live in the country between Abyssinia and Mombasa, and he thought that, as he could not reach the Galla through Shoa, he could do so from the eastern coast. He and his wife, accordingly, started from Aden in an Arab dhow; the vessel was nearly wrecked, and had to put back to Aden. A second attempt was more successful. On the 23rd of November, 1843, they started south again in a smaller dhow, under the command of a native from Mombasa. They made slow progress in the Gulf of Aden, and it was not until 18th December that they rounded the eastern horn of Africa. They then had a fairer wind, made a better voyage, and landed at Mombasa on 4th January, 1844.

Krapf immediately began to search for the most promising field for work. He made repeated excursions to Zanzibar, to secure the support of the Sultan, and to find the best site for his mission station. He finally resolved on Mombasa, where he settled in June. The natives of Mombasa have a proverb, "Better a useful infidel than a useless believer," and in that tolerant and practical spirit Krapf was welcomed. The Kadi of Mombasa at once helped Krapf in the translation of Genesis into Suahili. A month after the settlement,

Krapf lost his wife and his new-born child, and the bereaved missionary was left to work at his colossal task alone. He made an excursion into the country of the Wa-nyika, thinking that a mission there might be more useful than among the civilized Mohammedan people of Mombasa. He returned disappointed at the mental condition of the natives. "Drunkenness and materialism have completely blunted their perception of everything connected with spiritual religion," wrote Krapf; and he sadly confessed that among these people, "for the present, no great missionary results were to be obtained." But he had an unshaken belief that "Ethiopia shall soon stretch out her hands unto God."

To enable Christian missionaries to respond when the appeal came, Krapf translated the whole of the New Testament into Suahili, and compiled a grammar and dictionary of the language.

Next year (1845) he started inland again, to visit some Wa-kamba, hoping that they would be better disciples than the Wa-nyika, but he did not reach the Wa-kamba country, and returned to the Wa-nyika, who promised him every assistance. "Our land, our trees and houses, our sons and daughters, are all thine," said the elders, in reply to his request for permission to settle among them.

In 1845 Krapf was joined by Rebmann, the second of the two great missionary pioneers of Eastern Africa.

Krapf had arranged to found his station on the hills at Rabai, one of the spurs of the East African plateau, about ten miles from Mombasa. So Rebmann and he went together and asked the elders for the promised help. " The birds have nests, and 'the Wa-zungu [Europeans] too must have houses," replied the elders ; and the natives, though irregularly and unskilfully, gave the missionaries such materials as they had, and helped them to build their home.

There the two men laboured faithfully and patiently to teach the natives, to undermine the influence of the secret societies, and to abolish the old pagan rites. They secured a few converts, but only a few. The awful power of secret societies, the profound faith in fetishes, the reluctance of the natives to abandon the ceremonies connected with the initiation of boys into manhood, and their enjoyment of the orgies that accompanied the women's " Muansa," were all serious obstacles to the missionaries' success. Krapf and Rebmann worked on, undaunted by the difficulties of their task. Krapf learnt the language of the Wa-nyika ; he wrote a primer of its grammar, and collected much valuable information regarding the ordeals, institutions, and customs of the natives.

But the two missionaries sadly realized that they were making no sensible impression on the habits of the tribe, and they yearned for a people less drunken and less sensual than the Wa-nyika, and less influenced by Mohammedanism than the inhabitants of the coast towns.

Four days' journey inland from Rabai the missionaries

saw the rugged peaks of Kilibasi and Kadiaro rising above the plateau on their western horizon. The traders who knew the regions beyond these mountains told the missionaries weird stories of pygmies and cannibals, of white-capped, lofty mountains, of the "Second Sea," and of a vast western morass which is the end of the world. Little by little these stories though dismissed at first as "fabulous tales," had their influence: they roused in the two brave missionaries a keen interest in the western land.

Krapf had heard some of these stories before in Abyssinia, where he had been told of a dwarf tribe, the Doko; and apparently the same race were now reported to him by the east coast traders under the name of the Wa-bilikimo. But what especially interested the missionaries were the rumours of Christian tribes in the interior.

Krapf, when in Shoa, had heard of a tribe of white Christian Galla, and of the land of Kambat, "where a small nation of Christians, with fifteen churches and monasteries, is said to have retained its existence."

Hence, as the missionaries began to despair of the Wa-nyika, their thoughts turned to the people of the interior, and, in 1847, they definitely resolved to carry the Gospel to the inland tribes. It was decided that Rebmann should work due westward from Mombasa, while Krapf was to endeavour to reach his old goal, Galla-land.

The inland mission was begun in October, 1847, when Rebmann, with six Wa-nyika and two "Mohammedans" [Suahili], started on the first European expedition into the interior of British East Africa. The journey was short, and only lasted a fortnight: its goal was the peak of Kadiaro, some eighty miles west of Mombasa. Rebmann brought back such a favourable report of the mountain country, of the healthiness of its climate, and the friendliness of its inhabitants, that the two missionaries were eager to establish a station there. "As regards a mission," they wrote, "we can only say that it is very feasible and very desirable. The way is clear." And Krapf dreamed of a chain of mission stations stretching right across Equatorial Africa, from the Mombasa to the Atlantic shore.

A few months later Rebmann started inland again on a more ambitious errand. The missionaries had heard strange tales about Kilima Njaro, and Rebmann proposed to visit Chagga, the trading station at the south-eastern foot of the mountain. The Governor of Mombasa at first opposed the undertaking; he was reluctant to let Rebmann expose himself to such risks. "For," said he, "people who have ascended the mountain have been slain by the spirits, their feet and hands have been stiffened, their powder has hung fire, and all kinds of disasters have befallen them." Rebmann promised that he would not go "too near the fine sand," and left Rabai for the interior on 27th April, 1848. On

May 11, "about ten o'clock," he tells us in his journal, "I saw the summit of one of the peaks covered with a dazzlingly white cloud. My guide called the white which I saw, merely 'Beredi,' cold; it was perfectly clear to me, however, that it could be nothing else but snow." Rebmann returned to the coast, on June 11, to announce the discovery that Kilima Njaro is capped with perpetual snow.

In November of the same year Rebmann started on a third expedition, intending to reach Kikuyu; his party was larger, consisting of sixteen natives, armed, some with muskets, the rest with bows and arrows. The projected goal was not reached, but Rebmann paid a second visit to Chagga, and saw again, even by moonlight, the "majestic snow-clad summit" of Kilima Njaro. He learnt from the natives that the white material, when put into the fire, turns to water, and that its extent on the mountain varies with the season. In April, 1849, Rebmann tried again to penetrate beyond Kilima Njaro. He hired thirty porters, and hoped to reach the Unyamwesi country. It was the rainy season, and Rebmann, who travelled without a tent, often had no other protection than his umbrella. He reached Chagga, but the Chief extorted from him almost all his stores, and Rebmann was compelled to return to the coast.

While Rebmann was thus exploring to the west of Mombasa, Krapf had not been idle, and was preparing to fulfil his old dream of a mission to the Galla, whose

THE MOMBASA MISSIONS 61

land, in his enthusiasm, he describes as "Ormania, the Germany of Africa." He first had to make a short visit to the mountains of Usambara, in what is now German East Africa, and he travelled there with a party of one guide and seven porters. This mission accomplished, he felt at liberty to turn his attention to the north-west. His start was delayed by the arrival of Erhardt and Wagner, two recruits for the mission, who landed at Mombasa in June, 1849. Wagner died on the 1st of August, and Erhardt, for some time, was too ill and inexperienced to be left alone, so Krapf was detained for some months longer on the coast. At length, on the 1st November, 1849, Krapf was free to start on his projected mission. He read the 2nd chapter of Haggai, which strengthened him greatly, and leaving Rabai, he plunged into the dreary wilderness of the Nyika. His caravan consisted of twelve porters, and his immediate goal was Ukambani, the country of the Wa-kamba. Thence he hoped to work his way to the Unyamwezi, and onward "to the sources of the Nile, and to those still surviving Christian remnants at the Equator of whom I heard in Shoa."

The time was unfortunate, as it was the end of the long dry season; water was scarce, and the usual water holes dry; the route was badly selected, and took the party through scrub so thick that they had to crawl on hands and knees through the thickets. Nevertheless they crossed the Nyika in safety to Taita, whence

Krapf enjoyed a view of Kilima Njaro and its snow cap. Turning northward, he crossed the Tzavo River, and entered Ukambani. He reached the village of Kitui, and from a hill above it, on 3rd December, 1849, he saw the snow-flecked summit of Mount Kenya.

Krapf was delighted with the Wa-kamba, and resolved to establish a mission in their country. He secured the friendship of Kivoi, the chief of Kitui, and then returned to the coast for the necessary stores. Krapf's ultimate aim was to make this station in Ukamba the first in a chain of mission settlements extending across Equatorial Africa from Mombasa to the Atlantic.

He reached the coast in safety, and after a short rest marched inland with a caravan of thirty porters. Providentially, he fell in with a party of 100 Wa-kamba, who were returning home after a trading trip to Mombasa. In the Taita country the caravan was attacked by robbers. Krapf was no soldier, and always got into trouble when fighting began.

"In the confusion," he tells us, "I lost my powder horn, and one of my people burst the barrel of his gun by putting too large a charge into it. The ramrod of another was broken through his being knocked over by a Mnika [one of Krapf's own men], in the confusion, just as he was going to load, whilst the gun of another missed fire altogether." The Wa-kamba traders made a better defence, and beat back the robbers. Krapf was suitably modest over the victory. "It was God who preserved

THE MOMBASA MISSIONS

us," he says, "and not our own sword and bow"—a grateful acknowledgment, however, which omits direct reference to his Wa-kamba allies.

The rest of the journey was peaceful. Krapf reached the plateau of Yata on the eastern border of Ukamba, and there he built a hut and began mission work. He was greatly encouraged by the friendliness of the natives but troubled by the selfishness of his Wanika servants.

He visited his old friend Kivoi, who introduced him to a native from the southern slopes of Kenya. This man told Krapf that he had frequently been to the mountain, but had not ascended it, because it contained Kirira—a white substance producing very great cold. The white substance, he added, produced continually a quantity of water.

Kivoi was about to start for the country to the north of the Tana, and Krapf, delighted with the prospect of a nearer view of Kenya, consented to go with him.

Near the Tana the caravan was attacked by robbers. The first fight was a victory indirectly due to Krapf, though not to his fighting capacities. With characteristic simplicity he left his ramrod in his gun when he fired, so that he could not reload; but the enemy were temporarily routed by one of Kivoi's wives opening Krapf's umbrella. The raiders came on again later, and the caravan was defeated. Krapf, having provided himself with a new ramrod, fired twice, but he fired in the air, "for I could not bring myself to shed the blood of man," and then he joined in the general flight. Kivoi was killed, Krapf was left behind alone, and nearly fell into the hands of the enemy by mistaking them for his friends. He escaped, however, and hid in the forest on the Tana banks. There he prepared for his journey over the waterless desert, that lay between him and Ukamba. He filled his telescope and both the barrels of his gun with water, and started on the attempt to find his way back. His improvised water bottles were not a success, the telescope case leaked, and the bushes tore the grass plugs out of the gun barrels. He was soon starving for food and water. He ate leaves, roots, elephant dung, and ants; and when these failed, he tried gunpowder, and the bitter shoots of a young tree. " I soon felt severe pains in my stomach," says Krapf. The pains were probably very severe. Fortunately he fell in with two of his fellow fugitives, who guided him back to Ukamba. The natives were angry at the death of their chief, which they held that Krapf ought to have prevented. They appeared so hostile, that Krapf thought it prudent to escape. He tried to cross the country by night marches, but could not find his way, and after three days of terrible hardships, he threw himself on the mercy of a Mkamba. The native guided him to Kivoi's village, whence he was sent back to his station at Yata.

Worn out with his exertions, Krapf felt bound to return to the coast. The friendly Wa-kamba tried to persuade him to stay longer among them, but on his in-

THE MOMBASA MISSIONS

sisting, they consented to his departure, and he left, " not only in peace, but with honour."

So the first Ukamba mission failed by an unlucky accident, and Krapf returned to Europe in 1853, to recover from the effects of his nine years' work in British East Africa. In 1854 he started back for Rabai. He was stopped by severe illness in Egypt; he struggled with disease, and the indomitable old missionary would not easily give in. Reluctantly he was forced to the conclusion that his constitution was broken, and his African mission at an end. "So with deep sorrow," as we can well believe, "in August, 1855, I bade farewell to the land where I had suffered so much, journeyed so much, and experienced so many proofs of the protecting and sustaining hand of God, where, too, I had been permitted to administer to many souls the Word of Life and to name the Name of Jesus Christ in places where it had never before been uttered and known. God grant that the seed sown broadcast may not have fallen only in stony places, but may spring up in due season, and bear fruit a hundredfold."

But Krapf's African work was not yet done. In 1860 he published his journals. Their contagious enthusiasm roused some members of the United Methodist Free Church to help forward the work. They asked Krapf's advice. He, of course, offered his assistance, and urged them to undertake the work. In 1861 four missionaries—Wakefield, Woolner, and two Swiss

—were sent out to establish the Methodist Mission in East Africa. Krapf went with them to introduce them to the country, and help them to found their stations. Krapf took the Swiss to Kauma, in the northern part of the Wa-nyika country, a site he selected, as it was on the road to Galla-land. The missionaries were well received, and it was arranged that they should settle at Kauma as soon as they had learnt sufficient of the language. Wakefield and Woolner were then similarly introduced to the people of Usambara, and the mission prospects seemed bright. But a wave of anti-European feeling broke out in Mombasa, in consequence of a fight in the harbour between some Arab slaves and the boats of H.M.S. *Ariel*. The Swiss missionaries decided to return home, and Woolner accompanied them, as his health had collapsed.

Krapf then settled Wakefield at Ribe, a station six miles north-east of Rabai, where a year later Wakefield was joined by Charles New. These two missionaries faithfully strove to follow in the footsteps of Krapf and Rebmann. They worked among the Wa-nyika, and sought to increase the area of their usefulness by journeys inland. Wakefield, in 1865, visited the Galla at Chaffa, and New, in 1866, ascended the Tana Valley from Melindi as far as Ngao. He saw the Pokomo along the Tana, and visited the Galla at their villages on Lake Ashaka Babo. In 1871 New, whose interest in Kilima Njaro had been roused by an interview with

THE MOMBASA MISSIONS 67

Van der Decken, on that ill-fated traveller's return from the mountain in 1863, marched inland to Taveta. On the 26th August, 1871, in a second attempt to ascend Kilima Njaro, New settled for ever the controversy as to the character of its white cap by reaching its border, and actually handling the East African snow.

This mountaineering feat of New's was important, as the greatest doubts had been thrown on the truth of Krapf and Rebmann's reports. Neither of the missionaries was a scientific observer; they over-estimated their distances, and they miscalculated their bearings. Hence critics at home found it easy to detect improbabilities in their narratives. And one party of critics, headed by Livingstone and Cooley, scouted the possibility of these equatorial snows. Cooley's criticisms were the most precise: he declared that Kitui, the village whence Krapf saw Kenya, must "stand within 60 miles of the sea." The distance is really over 180 miles. The perpetual snows Cooley dismissed as a myth.

"With respect to those eternal snows, on the discovery of which Messrs. Krapf and Rebmann have set their hearts, they have so little of shape or substance, and appear so severed from realities, that they take quite a spectral character. No one has yet witnessed their eternity; dogmatic assertion proves nothing; of reasonable evidence of perpetual snow there is not a tittle offered. The only sentence in Mr. Rebmann's journal which ventures to touch upon the fact of a fall of snow is, as has been shown, neither genuine nor correct" (p. 127).

Livingstone was almost as contemptuous, and even in the introductory chapter to Krapf's own book the same doubts were expressed, for of Cooley's disbelief it is said, "whether on sufficient grounds or no is at best but doubtful."

Cooley not only denied the existence of the snow fields, but he attacked Krapf's character; he insinuated that his journeys were a misapplication of missionary funds to satisfy personal ambition.

"Krapf holds," says Cooley, "that in Africa, geographical discovery must precede evangelization, and it will be time enough to think of cultivating a corner of the immense vineyard when the whole of it shall have been explored. But the weakness of ambition is manifest in his blind attachment to grand problems, and his disinclination to relinquish the delusions connected with them. Miserably poor in facts, he is profuse of theory; his distances are exaggerated, his bearings all in disorder, his etymologies puerile, and he seems to want altogether those habits of mental accuracy without which active reason is a dangerous faculty."

These attacks on Krapf were unjust and unjustifiable. Fortunately the two founders of the East African Mission lived to see their reports confirmed, and their merits acknowledged.

After Krapf's return from the foundation of the Ribe

THE MOMBASA MISSIONS 69

Mission in 1863, he settled in Wurtemberg, whence he wrote bright messages of encouragement and hope, whenever the future of the East African Missions was especially gloomy. He lived to welcome Stanley's appeal for the evangelization of Uganda, and to strengthen those weaker brethren whose hearts misgave them, when the prospects of the Uganda Mission were at their worst.

Rebmann stayed on in East Africa, working patiently and faithfully, and almost forgotten. In 1872 Sir Bartle Frere found him at Rabai, blind and infirm, but still at work, and surrounded by a handful of devoted converts.

After the Freretown Mission was established at the end of 1874, Rebmann was reluctantly persuaded to return home. He consented, for he felt that his pioneer work was done. He had lived in East Africa, without a single break, from 1845 to 1874. He had maintained the continuity of the Church Missionary Society's work in East Africa, from the time of Krapf's departure till the mission of Sir Bartle Frere, and the re-establishment, in 1874, of the Society's work on a more adequate and worthy scale.

Rebmann was brought back to Europe, and settled beside his old comrade, Krapf, in the Kornthal. Krapf arranged his marriage with a pious widow, who nursed him through his last days.

But, after a twenty-nine years' residence in East

Africa, the return to Europe was too great a wrench. It would, perhaps, have been better for the blind old missionary to have died among the converts he had made, and to have been buried on the station where his life's work was done. Rebmann died within a year of his return, on 4th October, 1876, and five years later (26th November, 1881) Krapf followed him to his rest.

The story of the work of Krapf and Rebmann, the two founders of the East African Mission, is one of the brightest chapters in African history. They entered the mission field from motives of disinterested philanthropy. Their service is an example of the highest type of missionary enterprise. Their enthusiasm was irrepressible, and yet innocent of fanaticism; their sympathy with the natives they strove to convert was as deep as their patience was inexhaustible. They achieved great geographical success with insignificant resources. Though they did not hesitate to denounce evil practices, they kept aloof from politics; nevertheless they helped to revolutionize the political conditions of the continent by rousing European interest in Eastern Equatorial Africa. Their work was great, and their lives were noble. Said Said, the Sultan of Zanzibar, wrote the simple truth when introducing Krapf to the Governor of Mombasa, he described him as "a good man, who wishes to convert the world to God."

Chapter V

THE QUEST FOR THE NILE SOURCES

"Arcanum natura caput non prodidit ulli,
Nec licuit populis parvum te, Nile, videre,
Amovitque sinus, et gentes maluit ortus
Mirari, quam nosse, tuos. Consurgere in ipsis
Jus tibi solstitiis, aliena crescere bruma."
—*Lucan*, "*Pharsalia*" (x. 295–9).

Nature conceals thy infant stream with care,
Nor let thee, but in majesty, appear.
Upon thy banks astonish'd nations stand,
Nor dare assign thy rise to one peculiar land.
Exempt from vulgar laws thy waters run,
Nor take their various seasons from the sun.
—*Rowe's Translation.*

THE missionary was not long allowed a monopoly of pioneer exploration in East Africa. The philanthropist was soon joined by the geographical explorer. The annual occurrence of the floods of the Nile at the driest and hottest season of the year was an anomaly that impressed observers in all ages. Every attempt to solve this problem directly by a journey up the Nile Valley failed. The difficulties were long insuperable, and geographers turned their attention to the possibility of reaching the Nile sources from the East Coast. With this end in view, Ptolemy Philadelphus invaded Ethiopia ; and the accurate information of Ptolemy the geographer was doubtless derived from traders, who reached the Upper Nile basin from the Zanzibar coast.

The search for the Nile sources, in the present century, begins with the work of Sir Richard Burton, who, in 1854, was sent on a mission to Harrar, a town in the Galla country, south-west from Aden. The journey gave him a keen interest in African research ; and, a year later, he tried to make a dash for the interior from Berbera on the Somali coast. The attempt ended in disaster. The caravan was massacred by the Somali, Lieutenant Stroyan was killed, Speke escaped with nineteen spear wounds, and the Somali road was closed for thirty years.

When another opportunity to reach Central Africa came in Burton's way, he chose a more southern zone, and entered East Africa opposite Zanzibar. His former companion, John Hanning Speke, again went with him. The two travellers left the coast in June, 1857, and crossed the whole width of what is now German East Africa, to the eastern shore of Tanganyika.

This journey marked one of the great epochs in East African history, for it started the scientific explorations of the equatorial lakes. The honour of beginning this work belongs to the illustrious Burton ; the credit for its

THE QUEST FOR THE NILE SOURCES 73

continuation is mainly due to Speke. Burton was not the type of man to enjoy travel among the Bantu tribes of German East Africa. His mind was an unsuitable instrument for such rough work. His companion, the plodding Speke, though far inferior to him in brilliancy, made the more successful traveller in Eastern Africa. By the time the two men had reached the Arab settlement at Kazeh, on the journey home, Burton had had enough of the work. When Speke suggested a branch excursion to visit a reputed lake beyond the hills of Unyamwezi, Burton was only too glad to let his companion go alone, while he settled down for three months' life among the Arab traders. Speke left Kazeh on 9th July, 1858, and on the 3rd of the following month he reached the shores of the Victoria Nyanza.

It was this discovery which connects the Burton and Speke expedition with the history of British East Africa. The discovery was of fundamental importance, because it finally disposed of the theory that the various lakes reported by native traders were all based on one lake. Moreover, Speke claimed his lake as the true source of the Nile. Burton estimated the level of Tanganyika at 1,844 feet above the sea (it is really 2,750 feet); it was therefore improbable that it could be the source of the Nile, which, at 450 miles to the north of Tanganyika, is 450 feet higher. But Speke's Victoria Nyanza is at the level of 3,820 feet above the sea, and it was therefore quite possible that it might be connected with the Nile. Speke was confident that it was. " I no longer," he wrote, " felt any doubt that the lake at my feet gave birth to this interesting river." This discovery, however, was somewhat unlucky for Speke. It brought him at once into conflict with Burton and Livingstone, both of whom denied that the Nile rose in Speke's newly-found lake. Livingstone, in spite of inconsistent levels, derived the Nile from Tanganyika, and even denied the existence of Speke's lake as a fact. Geographers, at the time, mostly sided with Burton and Livingstone; and the cartographers broke up the Victoria Nyanza into a series of lakes and swamps.

To prove the existence of his newly-discovered lake and its connection with the Nile, Speke organized another expedition, in which he was accompanied by Grant. The expedition was well found, carefully organized and strongly escorted. It left Zanzibar on 2nd October, 1860. The caravan consisted of some men from the Cape Mounted Rifles, and 182 Zanzibari. The expedition followed Speke's old road to Kazeh, where it stayed two months for the reorganization of the caravan. After this point the difficulties began. The porters were so reduced in numbers that the caravan had to march thrice over every stage of the journey, and both explorers fell ill. The condition of the South African men was so precarious that they had to be sent home, and Speke accompanied them back to Kazeh. After he had rejoined Grant, the northward

THE QUEST FOR THE NILE SOURCES 75

march was resumed; but disaster still dogged the footsteps of the two explorers. The guides deserted, and once more Speke had to return to Kazeh to engage others. He secured two guides, but could get no more porters, and the caravan had to continue to work forward in detachments. While the force was thus divided Grant's section was attacked and his men scattered. With dogged perseverance, the two men steadily pushed northward. They crossed Uvinza and Usui, and reached the frontier of Karagwe, a province to the west of the Victoria Nyanza, now included in German East Africa.

Here there was a sudden change in the attitude of the natives. Speke and Grant were met at the frontier by officers carrying the royal maces of Karagwe. The officers bade them welcome in the king's name, the explorers were treated with universal respect, the caravan was supplied with food at the king's expense, and everything was done to help instead of to hinder. Speke and Grant had made an unexpected and important anthropological discovery.

The explorers had previously been travelling in a region ruled by ignorant petty chiefs, whose one idea was to get what they could for themselves by continual begging and theft. From the country of independent village communities, Speke and Grant had suddenly passed to the territory of a chief who ruled a large country in which his power was absolute, except where limited by the rules of a feudal system. The king, Rumanika, was hospitable, friendly and intelligent. Instead of plaguing the travellers by begging and bullying, he received them with great friendliness, and entertained them with princely hospitality. Speke was amazed at the change, both in the people and the conditions of travel. He describes Rumanika as "a model of good manners and good taste, and, in the truest sense of the word, a gentleman, ruling his people with justice, mingled, perhaps, with a little African severity."

The explanation of this startling change in his reception by the natives, and in the political conditions of the country, Speke rightly deduced from the physical characteristics of the Karagwe aristocracy. Speke describes Rumanika as a tall man, six feet two inches in height, "with nothing of the African in his appearance, except that his hair was short and woolly." Speke saw at once that the king and his courtiers were "as unlike as they could be to the common order of natives of the surrounding districts. They had fine oval faces, large eyes and high noses, denoting the best blood of Abyssinia."

Speke therefore concluded that an Abyssinian race had conquered some negro tribes around the Victoria Nyanza, and thus established the political system of Karagwe.

Speke's explanation is essentially correct. The race in question may not have been Abyssinian, but that the

THE QUEST FOR THE NILE SOURCES

semi-civilization of Karagwe was due to the influence of a non-negro race, which had conquered and ruled some negro tribes, is now universally accepted. Speke recognised this fact from the aspect of the people, and he obtained interesting evidence in its support from native traditions.

The explorers made a long stay at Rumanika's capital, where Grant was nursed through a serious illness. When his comrade could be safely left to the care of the king, Speke started for Uganda. He crossed the Kagera river, and from Meruka, on 3rd January, 1862, he obtained the first view of the western shore of the Victoria Nyanza. He followed the lake to the north, crossed Budu to Uganda, and reached the capital of the King Mtesa on 19th February, 1862. His reception in Uganda, as in Karagwe, was hospitable: the day after his arrival some pages drove in twenty cows and ten goats, with a request from the king that Speke " would accept these few chickens, until he could send more."

Speke was greatly impressed by the civil administration of Uganda, though horrified at the reign of terror and blood. Executions for the most frivolous reasons were a daily occurrence. The king, however, treated Speke well; and Grant, having recovered under Rumanika's care, arrived in May. In July the two explorers said farewell to Mtesa, who presented them with sixty cows, a flock of goats loads of butter, coffee and tobacco, and 100 sheets of bark cloth for clothing for the porters.

Illness soon forced Speke and Grant to part company once more. Grant's health collapsed, and he had to be left to journey slowly westward, while Speke went eastward to see the great river that was said to flow out of the Victoria Nyanza. On the 21st January he reached the river, and found it flowing northward. Speke followed it southward till he reached its outlet from the Victoria Nyanza at the "Ripon Falls." He then descended the river valley to the north, rejoined Grant, and the two explorers visited Kamrasi, the king of Unyoro. They then returned to the Nile, crossed to the right bank, and marched across the Shuli country, until they again reached the Nile, which they followed northward to Gondokoro. There, on the 15th February, 1863, they met Samuel Baker and Mrs. Baker, who had come in search of them; and in the Bakers' dhow they descended the Nile to Khartum.

This expedition of Speke and Grant showed that the Nile flowed from the Victoria Nyanza, but it did not conclusively prove either the unity of that lake, or that it was the only source of the Nile. Livingstone still insisted on dissecting the Nyanza into five lakes, and asserting that Tanganyika was the real southern source of the Nile. Speke and Grant, moreover, had themselves heard when in Unyoro of another lake into which the Nile flowed, between the point where they had left it

THE QUEST FOR THE NILE SOURCES 79

below the Victoria Nyanza, and where they rejoined it above Gondokoro.

In order, therefore, to complete the brilliant work of Speke and Grant, Samuel Baker and his devoted wife set forth on the expedition which discovered the Albert Nyanza. They had left Khartum in December, 1862, in order to meet Speke and Grant, and give them any assistance they might need. On the way up the Nile, they passed the steamer with the ill-fated party consisting of the Baronne von Capillan, her sister and daughter, Mlle. Tinné, two Dutch maids, a doctor, and an Italian, who were on their way to the Bahr-el-Ghazl, where they all died of fever, with the single exception of Mlle. Tinné. The Bakers were at Gondokoro when Speke and Grant arrived there in February, 1863; and at the end of March the Bakers started for the south. They followed the Nile to the falls near Lado, and then crossed to the eastern bank. They travelled across the Latuk and Madi districts, and reached the Nile again at the Karuma Falls. Thence they visited Mruli, the chief town of Kamrasi, king of Unyoro. Baker had some trouble with Kamrasi, who was a persistent beggar. However, he told Baker about the second Nile lake, which he called Mwutan Nzige, and sent men to guide him across Unyoro to visit it. Baker found the lake at the foot of some cliffs, 1,500 feet high, and so precipitous that he could not get his oxen down them. He describes the lake as in "a vast depression, far below the general level of the country, surrounded by precipitous cliffs, and bounded to west and south-west by great ranges of mountains from 5,000 to 7,000 feet above the level of its waters." Baker proved that the Nile flows into this lake from the Victoria Nyanza, and flows out again to the north. As it receives many streams from the south, it acts as a second reservoir for the Nile.

The Bakers' expedition, therefore, demonstrated the existence of the second of Ptolemy's Nile reservoirs. The true sources of the Nile had been found. But the solution of the Nile problem was still incomplete. The unity of the Victoria Nyanza had not yet been proved, and it was possible that some large rivers, worthy to be regarded as a continuation of the Nile, might flow into its southern end. That Tanganyika could discharge its surplus waters to the Victoria Nyanza was impossible; but when the lake levels were more accurately determined, the Albert Nyanza was found to be 300 feet lower than Tanganyika. Hence it was not impossible that Livingstone might be right after all, and that his favourite Tanganyika might be connected with the Nile.

These questions were not finally settled till the journey of Stanley ten years later, but Baker's results were generally regarded as conclusive. The inferences drawn from them have proved correct, and the Bakers' expedition to the Albert Nyanza practically closed the two thousand years' quest for the sources of the Nile.

Chapter VI

THE UGANDA ROAD AND THE TRAVERSE OF MASAI-LAND

"Mayo uazako, be ndo uendako."
"Where the heart desires, there it goes."
—*East African Proverb.*

THE expeditions, which discovered the Victoria Nyanza and subsequently proved its unity, reached the lake by what is now known as the "German road" to Uganda. This route begins on the coast opposite Zanzibar; it proceeds eastward across Usambara, and turns north across the country of the Wanyamwezi to the southern shore of the Nyanza. It is the road followed by Speke, Stanley, and the first missionaries to Uganda. New and Denhardt, however, had learnt from the Arab traders that there was a much shorter route, direct from Mombasa to the eastern shore of the Nyanza. Hence, as soon as European interest in Uganda was roused by Stanley's visit in 1875 (p. 107), the attempt to open up this road was eagerly discussed by geographers. There were two difficulties in the way.

The German road traverses inhabited country throughout its whole length; thus travellers can rely on food and water at every stage of the journey. The direct road, on the contrary, was known to cross wide belts that are uninhabited, and deserts that are uninhabitable. This difficulty, however, was a mere question of organization and transport; but the second and more serious difficulty was that this road crosses the country of the Masai, then the most formidable and dreaded tribe in East Africa.

That these difficulties were not insuperable was clear from the fact that the east coast traders had repeatedly crossed Masai-land. If native caravans, armed only with a few muzzle-loading guns made of second-hand Birmingham gas-pipe, and loaded with soft bullets and trade powder, could successfully travel and trade in Masai-land, it was surely possible for a well-organized European expedition, armed with breech-loading rifles, to explore the country.

Accordingly much attention was directed in Europe to the Arab trade route across Masai-land to the Victoria Nyanza.

The first explorer to show that this route was practicable to European travellers was a German naturalist, Dr. G. A. Fischer, who was sent out in command of an expedition organized by the Geographical Society of Hamburg.

Dr. Fischer started from Pangani, opposite Zanzibar

MASAI WARRIORS.

THE UGANDA ROAD

in 1882, with a caravan of 120 natives and porters, and accompanied by 100 extra men belonging to some native traders. He marched to Kilima Njaro, both the peaks of which were snow-clad, and early in 1883 he reached Little Aruscha—a village on the Masai border, previously visited by van der Decken. Beyond this point lay Masai-land, till then untrodden by Europeans. The Masai were, at first, hostile and aggressive, and while Dr. Fischer's porters were cutting firewood, they were attacked by some of the warriors or Elmoran. After a fight, in which two of the Masai were killed, the attack was repelled, and the expedition was allowed to advance. After a six weeks' journey, Dr. Fischer arrived at Ngurunani. On the 11th of May he reached Lake Naivasha, and was thus the first European to see the highest lake in the Erythrean Rift Valley. From Little Aruscha, where he entered Masai-land, to Naivasha is some 230 miles, and his last camp was only from 20 to 30 miles from the northern frontier, so that he had nearly traversed the whole of the widest part of the Masai country. His completion of the traverse was, however, impossible. Fischer had arrived at Naivasha at the most unfortunate time of year, when the Masai are usually massed around the lake. The natives were troublesome; they branded some of the porters with red-hot spears, and resolutely opposed Fischer's further progress to the north. His store of trade goods was exhausted, and he was taken ill, so he had to submit.

He stayed beside the lake for almost four weeks, and made a careful anthropological study of the Masai. He began his return journey on June 6th, and safely reached the coast at Pangani.

By this journey Fischer showed the practicability of the exploration of Masai-land, and his extensive scientific collections furnished important evidence as to the geological structure of the country. He obtained conclusive and unexpected proof of widespread volcanic action in the interior. He found hot springs in the Rift Valley: he saw a steam column rising from the summit of Doenyo Ngai, and heard that that volcano was in eruption in December, 1880. He saw snow on Kilima Njaro and Mount Meru.

Kenya was hidden from Fischer by the mountain Settima and the eastern wall of the Great Rift Valley. So the honour of confirming Krapf's report, as to the existence of a snow-clad mountain in British East Africa, was reserved for Joseph Thomson.

Thomson's expedition was organized and paid for by the Royal Geographical Society. The story of its adventures is graphically told in *Across Masailand*.

Thomson's caravan of 140 men left the coast on 15th March, 1883. He started from Mombasa, and crossed the Nyika to the Church Missionary Society's station at Taita, the first of Krapf's projected chain across the continent. Hence he continued westward to Taveta, on the south-eastern flanks of Kilima Njaro. He was warned there that it was impossible to enter Masai-land with less than 300 men, but he made the attempt. He found the Masai hostile, and returned to Taveta, where he joined forces with a company of Arab ivory traders, of whom the chief was the famous Jumbe Kimameta.

The caravan was now too powerful to fear direct attack, but Thomson was greatly bothered by the thievish and begging propensities of the Masai. "Even with our large caravan," he reports, "we had to submit with the meekness and patience of martyrs to every inconceivable indignity." The Masai warriors forced their way into the camp, though it was surrounded by a double thorn stockade. "In spite of everything," says Thomson, "they would frequently push the men aside and swagger into the tent, bestowing their odoriferous, greasy, clay-clad persons on my bed, or whatever object best suited their ideas of comfort. After formal salutations and assurances (with 'asides') of how delighted I was to see them, begging would commence, and string after string of beads would be given them in the hope of hastening their departure."

Notwithstanding these persecutions, Thomson and his companion Martin continued northward and reached Ngongo Bagas, at the south-western corner of the Kikuyu country. Here there was a fight between the caravan and the natives, resulting in the death of two porters and of several of the natives. After emerging from the Kikuyu forests, "the next march was a long one, without water, and ended in a marvellous scene of disorder and panic. Men fell down exhausted; lions attacked the donkeys, killing several. The donkeys fled braying, kicking off their loads, and, in the darkness, many were shot down as lions. Men threw down their loads, and fled for camp, or spent the night up trees. Lions roaring, donkeys braying, guns firing, shouts and cries of panic-stricken porters and excited masters, produced an effect such as I shall never forget, while fear-maddened cattle broke away from all control and crashed through the bush."

A three days' halt was necessary to repair the disasters of that night, and the caravan re-entered the Masai country and reached Naivasha. The Masai were very troublesome, and Thomson tells us that for ten days he literally bored his way through them, continually exposed to their plundering. He then crossed the northern flanks of Settima, in the hope of reaching Kenya, which he was the first European to see from the west. The Masai, however, were in force on Laikipia, the plateau which separates Settima and Kenya. Thomson, by tricks, gained a great reputation as a medicine man; but for which, he tells us, his progress would have been impossible. Even with this assistance he was "driven almost mad with days of worry and nights of incessant watchfulness."

At length Thomson's trade goods were exhausted,

and "as I had no better stock in hand than a couple of artificial teeth, and some Eno's Fruit Salt, to keep up my reputation as the Wizard of the North, my position became doubly dangerous." His food supply also failed, as one of those terrible epidemics of rinderpest, which periodically decimate the Masai herds, had recently broken out. "A strange disease," says Thomson, "had attacked the Masai cattle, and was sweeping them off in myriads. In many districts not a head was left, and our customary mode of travelling was, with fingers holding our noses, through miles of country covered with decomposing bodies. For the most exorbitant prices, we were able to buy nothing but bullocks, at the point of death. Of these only small portions were at all eatable, the rest being absolutely putrid, and even the bones were like mud. Such was our food in Laikipia." The attitude of the Masai became more hostile, and Thomson had "to take French leave at last, and fly in the middle of the night. We had almost to make a run of it, and having no loads, we soon put a considerable distance between ourselves and our persecutors." He fortunately escaped, reached the uninhabited, northern part of Laikipia, and began the descent to Njemps, the trading station near the southern end of Lake Baringo. On the way down Thomson got separated from his caravan, and had to find his way alone to Njemps.

Thence Thomson marched westward across Kamasia and Elgeyo, the plateau on the western side of the Rift

Valley. He entered Kavirondo, and reached the Victoria Nyanza in the district of Usoga, forty-five miles east of the outlet of the Nile.

Here Thomson was taken ill, so that he could not reach the Nile. He went north to Elgon, a great volcano, famous for its caves, which he described as artificial. On his way back to Baringo he was tossed by a wounded buffalo, but his injuries did not prevent his marching round Baringo, which he proved to be a small lake, disconnected from the Nyanza.

While staying at Njemps Thomson's health collapsed, and he had to be carried on a stretcher back to Naivasha. For two months he hovered between life and death in a miserable hut among the bamboos of Mianzini. His comrade, Martin, devotedly nursed him through the illness, and carried him to Ukambani. In that healthy district Thomson soon regained his health, and on 2nd June, 1884, he arrived in safety at the coast opposite Mombasa.

The results of Thomson's journey were of great importance. Thomson was the first explorer to cross the whole width of the Masai country and reach the Victoria Nyanza from the east. He had, moreover, shown that Lake Baringo was a small, isolated lake, whereas Denhardt's map had represented it as a long inland sea. The natives, however, persisted that, in addition to the small lake reached by Thomson, there was a much greater lake, which they called the lake of Samburu,

THE UGANDA ROAD

and that this was the lake marked on Denhardt's map as Baringo.

To settle the existence of the great lake of Samburu was the main object of the third great geographical expedition across Masai-land. It was commanded by Count Samuel Teleki von Szek, who was accompanied by Lieut. von Höhnel. The expedition was organized at Zanzibar, two years after Thomson's return. Teleki secured the services of Jumbe Kimameta, the trader who had helped Thomson across Masai-land, and as head man of his caravan, he took Dualla Idris, a young Somali, who had distinguished himself by his bravery during Stanley's march across Africa, and by his capacity as head man of the James and Lort-Phillips' expedition in Somali-land.

Teleki's caravan numbered 300 natives, and was exceptionally well provided with stores and trade goods. Teleki took with him 6,000 lb. of beads, 4,800 lb. of iron wire and cowries, and 80 loads of cotton cloth. The expedition left Zanzibar on 23rd January, 1887, and the march inland began from Pangani on 3rd February. It took the German road to Taveta, whence Kilima Njaro was explored and partially ascended. Teleki joined forces with a party of native traders, and the combined caravans entered southern Masai-land. To von Höhnel we are indebted for an account of the structure of this part of British East Africa. The explorers passed along Lake Nyiri, which must once have been far larger than at present, for between the lake and the mountains to the north-east are tracts of barren, sandy desert, covered with snow-white natron, which was deposited by the evaporation of the lake waters. Beyond Nyiri the country is richer, and the grass-clad steppes of the Kapte plains include some of the most populous districts of Masai-land.

On August 27th the expedition reached Ngongo Bagas, on the south-eastern corner of the Kikuyu country, where its most important work began.

The Kikuyu country is a narrow belt, some eight-and-twenty miles broad, extending from Ngongo Bagas on the south-west, to the slopes of Kenya on the north-east. The country is completely surrounded by a belt of dense forest, in the midst of which the inhabited district has been cleared. It has an elevation of 4,500 to 6,500 feet, and is well watered by many rivers, which flow through deep valleys to the south-east. Its soil is extremely fertile. Owing to the protection of the forest girdle, and the system of irrigation, the Kikuyu have been able to cultivate vast plantations, which are unusually well tilled and prolific. But before Teleki's journey this country was unknown. As von Höhnel correctly remarks, "Before our arrival little was really known about the land or the people of Kikuyu." No European had crossed the country. Fischer and Thomson had skirted its south-western border, but no tra-

THE UGANDA ROAD

veller had been allowed to enter the great plantations, which the Kikuyu religiously guarded from foreign intrusion. Teleki resolved to march along the middle line of the Kikuyu land, to the southern foot of Kenya.

With infinite trouble friendly relations with the Kikuyu were established. Teleki and some of the chiefs were made blood brothers, and the march began. Unluckily for the explorers they entered the country in September, the season when the sugar cane is ripe, and the natives have an abundance of intoxicating beer. Hence the warriors were drunk, and their insolent behaviour led to continual quarrels. For a week the strenuous efforts of Teleki and von Höhnel and of the leading local chiefs secured peace between the explorers' men and the drunken Kikuyu. But at length a native warrior wounded a porter with a poisoned arrow, and the Zanzibari fired a volley in reply. Seven of the Kikuyu chiefs, however, remained with Teleki, and took sides with him against their own people. In fact, faithful to the obligations imposed on them by blood brotherhood, the guides used to warn Teleki of any hostile designs.

After the first skirmish the natives divided into two parties, of which one was in favour of peace, while the other clamoured for war. The two factions became so angry that from argument they soon came to blows. At one conference, the peace party, suddenly closed up its ranks, and with a terrible war cry charged its opponents, and after a ten minutes' club fight drove the fighting faction from the field. Thanks to these energetic champions of peace, and the tact and forbearance of Count Teleki, there was a few days' respite, during which the explorers marched through a district, so carefully and systematically cultivated that it might have been in Europe. The natives were friendly, and in return for some strings of beads, used to supply the caravan with the thorn bushes with which the camp was defended at night.

The peace, however, was not permanent. On September 20th there was a fight with 2,000 warriors, who shot half a dozen arrows at the caravan, but fled, frightened at the noise of the wild firing of the excited porters. Ten days later, at Masiyoya, there was a more serious encounter. Teleki's patience was now exhausted, and he allowed his men to take decisive action. There was a sharp fight; the Suahili under Dualla attacked and burnt some villages, capturing a booty of 19 prisoners, 90 cows, and 1,300 sheep.

This encounter taught the Kikuyu better manners, and Teleki was supplied with food, and allowed to continue his journey without opposition. He left Kikuyu, and early in October pitched camp at Ndoro, at the western foot of Mount Kenya.

During a month's stay here, Teleki made the first partial ascent of the mountain. The chief difficulty was the passage of the bamboo zone, which consists of huge bamboos, growing as closely together as reeds. These would have been quite impassable, if a path had not been trodden through them by elephants and buffaloes; and, even as it was, "we often had to use the axe, and to part the bamboo stems, dripping wet with rain, with our outstretched arms—a most arduous and exhausting task."

Above the bamboo belt Teleki entered a zone of alpine meadows, from which he enjoyed the first near view of the Kenyan snow fields.

From Ndoro Teleki crossed the prairie country of Laikipia, which occurs as a wide, broad valley between Kenya and Settima, and expands to the north in a broad, open plateau. The caravan reached the eastern edge of the Rift Valley, and began the steep descent of its terraced precipices. The scenery was so magnificent that it moved the Zanzibari to raptures. One of them, Juma, was sent on to explore, and returned "in such wonderful good spirits," says von Höhnel, "that one would have thought he had been indulging in too much *bombe* (beer). He declared that his delight was merely at having caught sight of the gleaming surface of Lake Baringo." The descent was difficult; hills, which from the east appeared as mere inequalities of plain, were found to face the west with almost perpendicular precipices, from 650 to 1,000 feet in height.

The descent was successfully accomplished, and Teleki took up his quarters at the now well-known food centre of Njemps. The country, however, was suffering from famine, and the caravan had to stay there for more than two months, till grain supplies could be brought from the mountains, and stores of dried meat obtained from game. On the 10th February, 1888, Teleki and von Höhnel started north again, on the difficult march in search of Samburu.

They passed from Baringo and its fresh green sward to a desert, where storms buried the camp in sand and dust. They discovered a mountain chain, which they named after General (now Sir) Lloyd-Matthews, the Prime Minister of the Sultan of Zanzibar. The main difficulty was scarcity of water; the journey involved one stage of fifty miles, from a camp where a little water was obtained by digging in a stream bed, to the next water at the foot of Mount Nyiro. The guide engaged at Njemps and some of the porters were lost here; but after wandering for five days in the desert with nothing to eat but acacia gum, they managed to find the track of the caravan, and thus rejoin it.

From Nyiro it was but a short distance to the Lake of Samburu, but the approach to it was not encouraging. 'With every step, the scenery grew more and more dreary and deserted-looking. Steep, rocky slopes alternated with ravines, strewn with debris, which gave one the impression of being still glowing hot, and of having been but recently flung forth from some huge forge. . . . To the north, a single peak gradually rose before us, the gentle contours rising symmetrically from every side, resolving themselves into one broad, pyramidal mountain, which we knew at once to be a volcano. On the east of the mountain the land was uniformly flat, a golden plain lit up by sunshine, whilst in the east the base of the volcano seemed to rise up out of a bottomless depth, a void which was altogether a mystery to us. We hurried as fast as we could to the top of our ridge, the scene gradually developing itself as we advanced, until an entirely new world was spread out before our astonished eyes. The void down in the depths beneath became filled, as if by magic, with picturesque mountains and rugged slopes, with a medley of ravines and valleys, which appeared to be closing up from every side to form a fitting frame for the dark blue, gleaming surface of the lake, stretching away beyond as far as the eye could reach. For a long time we gazed in speechless delight, spellbound by the beauty of the scene."

On March 6th the explorers reached the lake, to find, to their bitter disappointment, that the water was brackish. Later travellers, such as Neumann, have found the Rudolf waters palatable and very pleasant to drink; but in 1888, either there must have been a failure of the rainfall to the north, which caused a lowering of the lake level, and consequent concentration of the salts in its waters, or else the mineral springs on the shore had, just before, been unusually active.

The lake water was rich in soda; it not only tasted like lye, but it effervesced strongly when tartaric acid was poured into it.

The situation was serious. "The full significance of the utterly barren, dreary nature of the district rose before the caravan like some threatening spectre. Into what a desert had we been betrayed! A few scattered tufts of fine, stiff grass, rising up in melancholy fashion near the shore, from the wide stretches of sand, were the only bits of green, the only signs of life of any kind. Here and there stood isolated skeleton trees, stretching up their bare, sun-bleached branches to the pitiless sky. No living creature shared the gloomy solitude with us; and far as our glass could reach, there was nothing to be seen but desert—desert everywhere. To all this was added the scorching heat, and the ceaseless buffeting of the sand-laden wind, against which we were powerless to protect ourselves upon the beach, which offered not a scrap of shelter, whilst the pitching of the tents in the loose sand was quite impossible."

Teleki, however, was determined to explore the lake. For a month the caravan marched northward along the eastern shore, tramping over sand deserts and lava plains; the porters daily grew weaker, owing to the purgative action of the soda-charged lake waters, and all the cattle died. Half way along the eastern shore, a clan of "Elmolo" were found living upon two barren sand banks in the lake; the two islands together are not a square mile in area, but upon them were huddled two villages of huts, with a population of some 150 to 200 people, who supported themselves by fishing. From these people Teleki got a small supply of food, and continued his march to the north. The water was still bad. "It tasted and smelt equally disagreeable, and to us Europeans was simply undrinkable," says von Höhnel. "The men were becoming so weak that Dualla's evening report was usually *watu wawili wamekufa* (two men have died)." Some of the porters went out of their minds, threw down their loads, and fled into the bush to die.

At length, on April 4th, "after fifty-four days' wandering in an all but uninhabited land, nearly bare of fresh water, and of vegetation, we were once more in a well-populated district," for the caravan found a tribe, the Reshiat, living in an alluvial plain at the northern end of the lake.

Teleki sojourned among these Reshiat for six weeks in order to rest his caravan. He occupied the time by a journey eastward to Lake Stephanie, a smaller, but still considerable lake, at a level of some 400 feet higher than Lake Rudolf. The lake at its southern end was very shallow, and so brackish that, but for the rain-pools, the caravan could not have remained beside it. That the saltness of the water was due to concentration by drought is probable, as the level of the lake was many feet lower than it had been when Teleki's Reshiat guide had last been there, three years previously. No satisfactory exploration of Lake Stephanie could be conducted, as there were no natives near the lake, and Teleki could obtain no food for his men. An attempt to return south along the western shore of Lake Rudolf was also foiled, and that route was first accomplished by a Suahili caravan from Mombasa a few years later.

Owing to the death of so many of his porters and baggage animals, Teleki's transport was seriously reduced. So on leaving the Reshiat he had to load his men with burdens of from 110 lb. to 148 lb. The porter's proper load is from 60 to 65 lb. Forced marches were necessary, and the caravan went 235 miles in sixteen days. At the southern end of Lake Rudolf, an active volcano was discovered and named by von Höhnel the Teleki Volcano.

To avoid the deserts on the eastern margin and floor of the Rift Valley, Teleki crossed to the west. He reached the country of the Turkana—a tribe of Nilotic negroes living on the plateau to the west and south-west of Lake Rudolf. The Turkana attacked the caravan, and were only repelled after a severe struggle. Food was unprocurable, and the caravan proceeded southward on the verge of starvation. Despite the Mohammedan horror of donkey-flesh, the men had to live on it; some wild fig-trees luckily supplied a few days' food, and enabled the caravan to reach the country of the Wasuk. The only foods available were wild berries and unripe grain (*dhurra*). So as rapidly as the feeble men could march, Teleki pushed southward. The Kerio was reached, and it was in flood. From sheer weakness some of the natives were drowned at the ford. Von Höhnel was taken seriously ill.

Teleki and Dualla roused the disheartened porters to continue their efforts; and at length, after an absence of 166 days, the exhausted remnant of the once powerful caravan reached its old camp at Njemps. Thence, after a long rest, the caravan returned to Mombasa, where it arrived on the 24th October, 1888.

By this important journey, Teleki had explored the last of the great African lakes that remained to be discovered; he had twice crossed the Masai country without conflict with the natives; and his assistant, von Höhnel, had mapped the whole length of the Rift Valley in British East Africa.

This expedition closed the work of the geographical pioneers in British East Africa. During Teleki's absence a great change had come over Eastern Africa. When he left for the interior, the country was a political no man's land. He reached Mombasa to find himself in a British Protectorate. The work of the missionary and of the geographical explorer had led to the usual consequences—the arrival of the European Consul, and the establishment of European control.

BOOK III

THE ESTABLISHMENT OF BRITISH CONTROL

"First the missionary, then the consul, then the general."
Oriental Proverb (*vide* Lord Salisbury).

Chapter VII

STANLEY AND THE UGANDA MISSION

"Work in the world must not consist entirely of the storage in museums of shells, and birds, and insects; and the Continent of Africa was never meant by the all-bounteous Creator to be merely a botanical reserve, or an entomological museum."—*Stanley.*

MANY different motives have reconciled men to the inconveniences of travel in British East Africa. Krapf believed it his duty to spread the Gospel news among the East African heathen. Fischer was a man of science, and felt himself adequately rewarded by scientific collections and anthropological discoveries. Thomson and Teleki, in addition to their geographical interests, were keen sportsmen, the former referring to his buffalo adventure as "one of those interesting episodes which enliven African travel and make the life endurable." But while the geographers were at work on exploration, a school of men was arising whose ideal was, in the best sense of the word political. Their aim was to improve the condition of the African native.

Samuel Baker was the first of these East African political geographers. As a young man he found his greatest joy in the killing of big game, and sporting interests led him to Africa, where his feats entitle him to rank as the greatest of the East African Nimrods. He visited the Nile tributaries of Abyssinia as a sportsman; his work there made him a geographer. He went to the Middle Nile to hunt, and passed thence to the Upper Nile to explore. There he found the country devastated by the slave trade, and he realized the pathos of savage life. He accordingly returned to Europe, resolved to devote his best energies to the rescue of the helpless agricultural tribes of the Eastern Soudan. From a geographer he had developed into a statesman.

The Austrian Mission had already been at work in the Upper Nile basin, but its results were disappointing. Baker saw that such efforts were premature. "Difficult and almost impossible," said he, "is the task before the missionary. The Austrian Mission has failed, and the stations have been forsaken; this pious labour was hopeless, and the devoted priests died upon their barren field." Missionaries can only work, with reasonable hope of success, where natives enjoy security against attacks by the slaver and the raider. "The sower knows not who will reap, thus he limits his crop to his bare necessities." Accordingly Baker declared "that the first step necessary, in the improvement of the savage tribes of the White Nile is the annihilation of the slave trade. Until this be effected, no legitimate commerce can be established, neither is there an opening for missionary enterprise; the country is sealed and closed against all improvement."

But Baker also realized the fact, which has been overlooked by many of the anti-slavery advocates, that to suppress slavery without establishing anything in its place would be useless, even where it would be possible. Slavery is so woven into the social system of Eastern Africa, that its removal without a substitute would be the industrial ruin of the country. Intertribal trade is necessary to the well being of the natives. They want iron weapons and tools, better domestic appliances, and more economical methods of agriculture. What is wanted for the salvation of Africa, said Baker, is "honest trade." "If Africa is to be civilized, it must be effected by commerce, which, once established, will open the way for missionary labour."

Baker therefore offered his services to the Khedive, and returned to the Upper Nile with a commission to reorganize the Egyptian provinces in the Soudan, suppress slave raids, and introduce better administrative methods than those of the ordinary Pasha.

Baker's rule in the Soudan, however, rarely brought him in direct contact with British East Africa. His successor, Gordon, at one time intended to annex Uganda to the Egyptian provinces, and sent missions there. But the influence of both men on British East Africa was indirect. The real foundations of European rule in Eastern Equatorial Africa were laid by H. M. Stanley.

Stanley's work in Equatorial Africa began in 1871, when he was sent by the *New York Herald* to discover whether Livingstone were still alive, and, if so, to furnish him with fresh supplies. He started on this quest, as he himself has told us, with feelings of indifference. His first impressions on meeting Livingstone were undeniably those of disappointment, and for some time he was more bored than interested. He listened politely to an exposition of Livingstone's theory of the Central African river system. According to this theory, the river at the northern end of Tanganyika flowed out of the lake. The Ujiji Arabs, however, declared that it flowed into the lake. The river was easily accessible, so the practical Stanley resolved to go and see. He engaged guides, arranged an expedition, and invited Livingstone to accompany him as his guest. The two explorers travelled together round the lake to its northern end, and found that the Arabs' statement was correct.

This short journey settled a great deal more than the flow of the Ruzizi. Round the camp fires at night Livingstone told Stanley the story of his life and wanderings, and gradually roused in the young journalist a deeper respect for abstract knowledge than he had felt before. Stanley returned to the coast, leaving Livingstone

HENRY M. STANLEY, AT THE TIME OF HIS FIRST EXPLORATIONS IN AFRICA.

to continue his explorations to the west of Lake Tanganyika. Two years later Livingstone died, leaving his work unfinished.

Meanwhile, the interests which Livingstone had roused in Stanley were growing. After Livingstone's funeral in Westminster Abbey in 1874, Stanley was fired with the resolution to complete the work in which his teacher had fallen. Mr. Gordon Bennett and the *Daily Telegraph* gave him the money, and he was soon back on the East Coast, his life dedicated to African service.

Stanley's interests were twofold. He was anxious to solve several geographical problems. He was ready "to be, if God willed it, the next martyr to geographical science." But he was still more anxious to ameliorate the lot of the African native. He had undertaken, nominally as his second, but probably as his main object, "to investigate and report upon the haunts of the slave traders."

Stanley arrived at Zanzibar on this mission in 1874, he spent seven weeks in organizing his caravan, and he left Bagamoyo, on the 17th of November, at the head of a force of 356 men. His first aim was to sail round the Victoria Nyanza in order to settle the question whether it were one lake or a group of lakes. He marched to the southern shore of the Nyanza, taking with him the sections of a boat, which he launched on the lake at the end of February, 1875. On the

8th of March he started on his memorable circumnavigation of the Victoria Nyanza. The cruise was remarkably successful. Stanley proved thereby the unity of the Victoria Nyanza, and showed that no river of a size corresponding to the Nile flows into the lake; he saw the outlet of the Nile over the Ripon Falls, and he heard of the volcanoes of Masai-land—low hills which discharge smoke and sometimes fire from their tops. Geographically, therefore, the results were important; but politically, they were more important still.

To understand the political results of Stanley's voyage, we must remember one ethnological fact. South of a line across Equatorial Africa, from the Cameroons on the west to the mouth of the Juba on the east, the natives belong to the group of negroes known as the Bantu. A few of the tribes, such as the Zulu and their offshoots the Mtabili, have acquired an organized military system. But, as a rule, the Bantu live in independent village communities ruled by petty village chiefs or committees of elders. The villages, or small groups of villages, are isolated and usually hostile to their neighbours; and, as there is no union between the independent clans, they are weak and at the mercy of any band of organized slave raiders that attack them. While Stanley was marching from Bagamoyo to the Victoria Nyanza, he passed through typical Bantu districts, and saw no opening for any effective help till he arrived in Uganda, at the northern end of the

STANLEY AND THE UGANDA MISSION 109

Victoria Nyanza. Here he found a more hopeful condition of things.

In Uganda the basis of the population consists of some tribes of primitive Bantu. But these aborigines have been conquered by a higher race, which does not belong to the negro stock, and is allied to the race now dominant in Abyssinia. The conquerors of Uganda, the Wahuma, invaded the country from the north-east, and established in it an organized, centralized government. The non-negro Wahuma have, in fact, done for Uganda, what the Romans and the Normans did for England.

Speke and Stanley have both collected traditions of the settlement of the Wahuma in Uganda. According to Stanley's version, the first king was Kintu, who migrated to Uganda in about the thirteenth or fourteenth century. He took with him his wife, a cow, a goat, a sheep, a banana root, and a sweet potato. He found Uganda uninhabited and so settled there. His wife gave birth annually to four children of such miraculous precocity that the girls, when two years old, gave birth to other children, who, in turn, had families at an equally early age. Kintu's sons prepared for themselves strong drink from the banana, and under its influence, indulged in wild debauchery. At length they threatened to kill their parent. Kintu, distressed at the wickedness of his family, withdrew to the spirit-land. He was succeeded by his son, Chewa, who organized a search for his father, which continued for several generations. Among Chewa's successors was Kimeia, the mighty hunter, whose feet trod holes in the rocks; he was a model king, and made Uganda an ordered state. After him came Nakwingi, who conquered Unyoro, and the brave Kamanya, who subdued the ferocious Wakedi. Finally, as the thirty-fifth king after Kintu, came Mtesa, who was reigning at the time of Stanley's visit.

During his march to the Victoria Nyanza, Stanley had experienced the usual annoyances of travel among the northern Bantu. He had had to buy food for his caravan by retail, two or three pounds at a time, and to haggle over the price to resist extortion; he had to be ever on the alert to protect his camp from the attack of thieves, and his porters from being speared if they loitered behind the caravan. During his voyage round the lake he had a desperate encounter with the people of Uvuma, then the pirates of the Nyanza.

On Stanley's entrance to Uganda he found the conditions strikingly different from those of the country to the south. The civility of the natives, their ungrudging hospitality, and their implicit obedience to the orders of the king, showed a political system superior to anything among the unorganized Bantu. As soon as Stanley entered Uganda, while journeying to see the king, he realized, as he tells us, "that we were about to become acquainted with an extraordinary monarch and an extraordinary people, as different from the barbarous pirates of Uvuma and the wild, mop-headed men of Eastern Usukuma, as the British in India are from their Afridi fellow-subjects, or the white Americans of Arkansas from the semi-civilized Choctaws."

Stanley had been to some extent prepared for the contrast between Uganda and the Bantu countries to the north by the accounts of his predecessors. But he expected trouble from the king, Mtesa, whom Speke and Grant had described as a vain, dissipated, bloodthirsty tyrant. Stanley, however, was welcomed with a friendly greeting and a princely gift of food. This cordial reception was at first regarded as sufficiently explained by a dream of the king's mother. Mtesa told Stanley that "his mother dreamed a dream a few nights ago, and in her dream she saw a white man on this lake in a boat coming this way, and the next morning she told the Kabaka [the king], and lo, you have come."

The improvement in Mtesa's behaviour, however, was not due solely to a dream. When Speke was in Uganda, it was the rule that there should be one execution daily, so men and women were butchered for the most trivial offences. To touch the king's clothes, even by accident, to look upon the king's wives, to expose an inch of leg when sitting on the ground, or to disarrange the bark cloth robe, which is the national dress, were capital offences. During an excursion that Speke made with Mtesa, one of the king's many wives offered her husband some fruit she had plucked off a tree; for her audacity in venturing to offer the king food the woman was ordered to immediate execution, and her life was only saved by Speke's intercession. "Nearly every day," says Speke, "incredible as it may appear to be, I have seen one, two, or three of the wretched palace women led away to execution, tied by the hand, and dragged along by one of the body guard."

This reign of passion and terror was at an end, and Stanley found that the change was due to the teaching of a Moslem missionary, Muley bin Salim. Mtesa was a different man from the monster described by Speke. "The king's character," says Speke, "was a mixture of childish frivolity and uncontrollable passion." Stanley found him a dignified, intelligent king, who ruled his country with justice, and had learnt to curb his own capricious will.

Mtesa was described in Stanley's first despatch from Uganda to the *Daily Telegraph*, as unlike the negro, and resembling "the Muscat Arab when slightly tainted with negro blood." Stanley was captivated at once by his manner, "for there was much of the polish of a true gentleman about it; it was at once agreeable, graceful, and friendly."

In a more detailed subsequent description, Stanley tells us that "the Kabaka (king) is a tall, clean-faced, large-eyed, nervous-looking, thin man, clad in a tarbush, a black robe, with a white shirt belted with gold. He has very intelligent and agreeable features, reminding

A GROUP OF UGANDA NATIVES.

me of some of the faces of the great stone images at Thebes. He has the same fulness of lips, but their grossness is relieved by the general expression of amiability, blended with dignity, that pervades his face, and the large, lustrous, lambent eyes, that lend it a strange beauty, and are typical of the race from which I believe him to have sprung. His colour is of a dark red brown, of a wonderfully smooth surface."

The political condition of Uganda under Mtesa had improved, and Stanley found the country ruled by a feudal system, which, in comparison with the isolated village system of the Bantu tribes, was an advanced civilization. The king's word was law throughout his dominions; roads traversed the country in every direction; causeways had been built across the swamps; justice was dispensed through a regular judicial system, in which the king, aided by his councillors, acted as the supreme judge; the revenues were derived from tribute paid by subject chiefs; the palace was protected by a guard of 3,000 disciplined warriors, and was attended by a court of a hundred chiefs, as well armed and clad as the Arabs of Zanzibar and Oman.

Mtesa had an army of 150,000 soldiers, and a navy of 325 canoes, of which the hundred largest carried a crew of fifty men apiece.

Stanley at once grasped the possibilities of Uganda. He saw that it could be used as a centre for the civilization of the surrounding countries. His first idea was to civilize the country by trade. "Oh, for the hour," he exclaimed, "when a band of philanthropic capitalists shall vow to rescue those beautiful lands." But Stanley realized that Uganda could not pay commercially. It had no Congo connecting it with the East Coast, and it yielded no sufficient quantity of any commodity valuable enough to maintain a considerable European trade.

There was a second motive, however, to which an appeal could be made. The religious zeal which had civilized the rough forests of the north could carry salvation to the malarial swamps of the Equator. If, thought Stanley, Islam could have wrought so great an improvement in Mtesa since Speke's visit, Christianity could do yet more; Mtesa might be "the possible Ethelbert, by whose means the light of the Gospel may be brought to benighted Middle Africa," if only Europe could supply an Augustine.

"Mtesa has impressed me," he wrote, "as being an intelligent and distinguished prince, who, if aided in time by virtuous philanthropists, will do more for Central Africa than fifty years of Gospel teaching, unaided by such authority, can do. I think I see in him the light that shall lighten the darkness of this benighted region. In this man I see the possible fruition of Livingstone's hopes, for with his aid the civilization of Equatorial Africa becomes possible."

Stanley resolved to appeal to England for missionary

help; and to secure a friendly reception to any missionaries who might go to Uganda, he set to work to replace Mtesa's faith in Islam by faith in the doctrines of Jesus of Nazareth.

Stanley translated the Gospel of St. Luke, and wrote an abridgement of the Bible in a language Mtesa could read. In his business-like way he then proceeded to convert the king. He told Mtesa the story of Christ so earnestly and effectively that the king renounced Islam, ordered the Christian sabbath to be kept throughout Uganda, and promised to build a church. He had the Ten Commandments, the Lord's Prayer, and the commandment, "Thou shalt love thy neighbour as thyself," written in Arabic upon a board, and hung in the Palace, so that all his court might see it daily; and as a practical commentary on the text, he pardoned some condemned rebels at Stanley's request.

Finally, Mtesa begged Stanley to stay in his country to educate the people. Stanley knew that Mtesa's conversion was very imperfect, and that the evil habits of thirty years could not be cured by a few months' work. To make the conversion complete and real the residence of a permanent missionary in the country was necessary. Stanley could not accept Mtesa's invitation for himself, but he promised to persuade some English missionaries to settle in Uganda. To prepare the way for them, and help them when they arrived, he left behind an English-speaking native Christian, who had been trained in a mission station on the coast. Then he sent home a glowing description of Uganda as a mission field, and an impassioned appeal to Christian England to send out a suitable missionary. He sketched, moreover, the sort of man who was wanted.

"What a field and harvest ripe for the sickle of civilization! It is not the mere preacher, however, that is wanted here. The bishops of Great Britain collected, with all the classic youth of Oxford and Cambridge, would effect nothing, by mere talk, with the intelligent people of Uganda. It is the practical Christian tutor, who can teach people how to become Christians, cure their diseases, construct dwellings, understand and exemplify agriculture, and turn his hand to anything— this is the man who is wanted. Such an one, if he can be found, would become the saviour of Africa. He must be tied to no church or sect, but profess God and His Son and the moral law, and live a blameless Christian, inspired by liberal principles, charity to all men, and devout faith in Heaven. He must belong to no nation in particular, but to the entire white race."

Stanley's letter was entrusted to Lieutenant Linant de Bellefonds, a French officer in the Egyptian service, whom Gordon sent on a mission to Uganda while Stanley was there. Linant was killed on his return journey, but the letter was found by accident and sent on to England, where it arrived in November, 1875. It was received with coldness by many men, such as Lord

STANLEY AND THE UGANDA MISSION 117

Lawrence, who were of great influence in the missionary world. Stanley was unpopular, and was distrusted by English society. In some quarters the letter was treated as a joke; the *Saturday Review* saw the humour of an alliance between the *Daily Telegraph*, the *New York Herald* and Mr. Stanley on the one side, and the Church Missionary Society on the other.

But the letter arrived at a time when Europe was taking an especially keen interest in African work. A mission settlement for freed slaves had just been established on the eastern coast opposite Mombasa. Gordon's work in the Soudan was being watched with eager interest, and Stanley's powerful appeal deeply moved the British public. A great meeting was held in Exeter Hall; Mtesa's invitation was accepted; the necessary funds were soon subscribed; and a party of missionaries left London for Uganda.

The first Uganda Mission consisted of six men, under the command of a retired naval lieutenant, Shergold Smith. The party left England in the spring of 1876. It was delayed on the eastern coast of Africa, and it was not until May, 1877, that four members of the party reached Stanley's old camp on the southern shore of the Nyanza. There the doctor died, and O'Neill was left to superintend the building of a native boat. Lieutenant Smith and the Rev. C. T. Wilson crossed the lake to Uganda, where they were warmly welcomed by Mtesa. Smith returned to bring up more stores and men, but he and

O'Neill were killed by the natives of Ukerewe, an island on the lake, owing to a dispute over the purchase of a boat. The news of this succession of disasters discouraged the friends of the Uganda Mission at home; but they were inspired to renewed efforts by Mtesa's welcome, the faith of the English people, and the veteran Krapf's confident assurance of success. "Though many missionaries may fall in the fight," wrote Krapf, "yet the survivors will pass over the slain in the trenches, and take this great African fortress for the Lord."

Four more missionaries were accordingly sent to Uganda by the route up the Nile. In the meanwhile Wilson, who had been left alone by Smith in Uganda, had left for the southern end of the lake, as he did not get on very well with Mtesa. Here in August, 1878, he was joined by A. M. Mackay, the last member of Shergold Smith's party, and together they returned to Uganda, where, after suffering shipwreck and other adventures on the way, they landed on November 1st, 1878. Wilson left the same month to meet the missionaries who were coming up the Nile, and Mackay remained in charge of the Mission station at Mtesa's capital, Rubaga. Mackay soon acquired great influence over Mtesa, and, by February 14th, 1879, when Wilson returned with three of the recruits, the position of the Mission had been greatly strengthened. Wilson and Felkin returned at once to England with some envoys

STANLEY AND THE UGANDA MISSION

from Mtesa, leaving Mackay, Litchfield, and Pearson to carry on the evangelization of Uganda.

The English Mission was now well established; there were three missionaries at work; the king was friendly, and though the Mohammedan party were jealous, it could do nothing against the missionaries while the king was on their side.

The situation was suddenly changed by the appearance of a new and unexpected factor. Stanley's appeal to Christian Europe to evangelize Uganda had been only too successful. For a week after Dr. Felkin and his colleagues reached Rubaga, the capital of Uganda, there arrived two Catholic missionaries belonging to the order of the White Fathers of Algeria.

The newcomers were white men; they were Christians; they had come in response to Stanley's appeal. So they were welcomed by Mtesa. There was immediate friction between the Catholic and Protestant missionaries, which culminated in a deplorable quarrel in Mtesa's presence at a religious service that was being conducted by Mackay. Père Lourdel called the Protestant Bible "a book of lies"; Mackay made some remarks about the Virgin Mary and the Pope. Mtesa was bitterly and genuinely disappointed. The curse of Uganda had been faction feuds, in which religious quarrels have played a leading part. Apparently, Mtesa's main motive in wishing to Christianize his country was, by the introduction of a new and peace-teaching religion, to oust the rest. As soon as he found that the Christian missions divided into two hostile parties, and thus intensified religious feuds instead of healing them, Mtesa regarded Christianity as useless to him. "Every white man has a different religion. How can I know what is right?" asked the puzzled king.

Accordingly, he told both parties of missionaries to return to Europe, and there decide which was the true religion, and, when they had settled that problem between themselves, they could come back and tell him, and he would believe them. But until then he had no more use for either of them.

The missionaries were not expelled, for Mtesa was still faithful to his promise to Stanley. He continued to supply them with food and to protect them. But the chance for the Christianization of Uganda had been lost. The king was now indifferent; the Mohammedans could be openly hostile, and Christianity made no substantial progress during the rest of Mtesa's rule.

Luckily for the missions, however, Mtesa soon afterwards quarrelled with the Mohammedans. They incensed the king by refusing meat from his table, because it had not been killed according to Mohammedan rites. The fastidious Mohammedans declared the meat was not fit for dogs, and many of them were executed for this injudicious expression of opinion. Hence the Christian missions gained some ground.

The Catholics claim to have secured most of the

converts, and so the native hostility was mainly directed against their mission. Their position became unbearable, and in 1882 they withdrew to the southern shore of the Nyanza. Mackay and two other members of the Protestant mission stayed on, but they had to act with the greatest caution.

In 1884 Mtesa died, and was succeeded by Mwanga a son chosen owing to having such close physical resemblance to Mtesa, that his paternity was free from doubt. Mwanga was jealous of the Europeans, and resolved to get rid of them. He arrested the missionaries, and began a persecution of the native converts, three of whom were burnt to death in January, 1885. The persecution, however, was at first intermittent, and the missionaries were soon released.

Next year matters were brought to a crisis by the approach of Bishop Hannington along that road to Uganda, by which, according to native tradition, the future ruler of Uganda should come. Protests against the Bishop's choice of this route were made, both in England by Joseph Thomson, and in Uganda by the missionaries. So strong was the feeling in Uganda, that Mackay promised Mwanga that the Bishop should not enter Uganda by the road, but by canoe across the lake; and he sent an emphatic message to this effect to the Bishop. The warnings, however, were disregarded; it is possible that Mackay's miscarried. Hannington pushed ahead of his caravan with forty men, and reached the village of Lubwas, on the eastern bank of the Nile. Here he was detained by the chief, until orders respecting him came from the king. They came, and Bishop Hannington and his forty men were murdered on October 22nd, 1885.

This event closed the direct eastern road to Uganda for some years. It led to still greater difficulties in the position of the missionaries in Uganda. Mwanga felt that he had sinned beyond forgiveness, and the persecution of the native converts was renewed. Missionary work was rendered impossible, and all the Europeans left Uganda, except Mackay, who remained alone in the country for a year. In July, 1887, he too followed his colleagues, and it seemed as if the failure of the Uganda Mission, which had begun work ten years before with brilliant promise, was final and complete.

Chapter VIII

THE BRITISH EAST AFRICA COMPANY AND THE STRUGGLE FOR WITU

Hamlet. Goes it against the main of Poland, sir,
         Or for some frontier?
Captain. Truly to speak, and with no addition,
         We go to gain a little patch of ground
         That hath in it no profit but the name.
         To pay five ducats, five, I would not farm it;
         Nor will it yield to Norway or the Pole
         A ranker rate, should it be sold in fee.
Hamlet. Why, then the Polack never will defend it.
Captain. Yes, 'tis already garrisoned.
Hamlet. Two thousand souls, and twenty thousand ducats
         Will not debate the question of this straw.

IN the last chapter we have seen that Stanley's visit to Uganda in 1875 led to the introduction of two rival bands of missionaries. Their settlement altered the political conditions of the country, for the Protestants were armed with letters from the British Foreign Office which, they claimed, gave them a semi-official position. But Stanley's first journey across Africa was attended by more immediately important political results than the foundation of the Uganda Mission. It was the direct cause of the chain of circumstances, which led to the division of tropical Africa among the European Powers. This partition has had such a profound effect, not only on Africa, but on Europe, that Stanley's journey must rank with Columbus' voyage to America, and Vasco da Gama's discovery of the Cape route to India, as the three geographical achievements that have most deeply affected the politics of the world.

At the end of Stanley's visit to Uganda, he returned to his camp on the southern shore of the Victoria Nyanza. Thence he turned westward to a region where the need of civilizing influences was more urgent than in Uganda. He arrived on the banks of the Lualaba, which had been previously reached by Livingstone and Cameron. It was still unknown, however, whether the river was the head stream of the Congo or of the Nile. The seventeenth century geographers (see *e.g.* Sanson's map, p. 48) represented it as the upper part of the Nile; and the nineteenth century authorities, under the influence of Livingstone and Burton, generally accepted the same view. Previous efforts to settle the question by following the Lualaba to the sea had failed. The difficulties were appalling, but Stanley overcame them all; he left the last of his three European comrades dead upon the way, and with the remnants of his caravan he reached the Atlantic at the mouth of the

THE BRITISH EAST AFRICA COMPANY 125

Congo. He thus settled the last of the great geographical problems connected with the sources of the Nile, and the river system of Equatorial Africa. But the political results were even more important than the geographical. Stanley found the magnificent waterway of the Congo used only by Arab slavers and their allies for attacks on the weak and industrious tribes. He saw the terrible plight of the Congo natives, and returned home to organize a mission for their protection. Like a modern Peter the Hermit, he preached a crusade through Europe and America, and persuaded the King of the Belgians to join him in the adventure. An International African Association was established, and Stanley returned to Africa in 1879 to found the Congo Free State.

The Free State was established from philanthropic motives. "I am charged," wrote Stanley, "to open, and keep open if possible, such districts and countries as I may explore, for the benefit of the commercial world. The mission is supported by a philanthropic society, which numbers noble-minded men of several nations. It is not a religious society; but my instructions are entirely in that spirit. No violence must be used, and wherever rejected the mission must withdraw to seek another field."

In that spirit the organization of the Congo Free State was begun. Stations were built, missions established, and a considerable trade sprang up. After five years' successful work, Stanley returned to England for a rest, leaving the country ruled by a band of young heroes, such as the American Glave, the Englishman Deane, and the Belgian Coquilhat, working together in a spirit of self-sacrificing devotion.

The fair promise of those early years led to a very exaggerated idea of the commercial value of the interior of Africa; and this view had wide-reaching results. Germany was keenly feeling the loss of her subjects by emigration; her statesmen were beginning to realize the possibility of a commercial union of the British Empire, which would exclude German manufactures from the British Colonies. Increasing military expenditure rendered her increasingly dependent on her manufactures. German statesmen and commercial men were accordingly anxious to found a colonial empire of their own. The Monroe doctrine kept them out of South America; Asia was all occupied; Africa only was left. Bismarck, regarding English friendship as essential to his policy in Europe, allowed nothing to be done that might jeopardize his relations with England. He damped the ardour of the German colonial party until, after some fencing with Lord Granville, he knew that England would only make Platonic protests so long as English colonies were not directly touched.

As soon as Bismarck's mind was clear on this point, he allowed a step to be taken which precipitated the partition of Africa among the European Powers.

THE BRITISH EAST AFRICA COMPANY

The German flag was hoisted first on the western coast of South Africa, and then on the eastern coast, opposite Zanzibar. German agents had repeatedly visited the eastern coast, between 1880 and 1885, and made treaties with various chiefs in the interior. These treaties were unofficial until after 17th February, 1885, when the German Kaiser granted his charter of protection to the Society of German Colonization, which acquired these treaty rights. England at once protested against any step which would interfere with the independence of the Sultan of Zanzibar, or with the vested commercial interests of the many British Indian merchants who had trading stations and plantations in Zanzibar and along the coast. British intervention in the dispute between Germany and Zanzibar was justified by the position created by Lord Canning's award, which settled East African affairs after the death of the Sultan Said Said at sea in 1856. Said's sons quarrelled as to the division of their heritage, and the dispute was referred for arbitration to Lord Canning, then Viceroy of India. By his award, Zanzibar was declared independent of Oman, and the East African coast was assigned to Zanzibar. In lieu of his African possessions the Iman was awarded an annual subsidy, to be paid by India. This payment placed Zanzibar in the position of a subsidized dependency of India. Accordingly the German Government declared that it had no intention of interfering with the Sultan of Zanzibar, and that the territories, which its agents had acquired, lay 100 miles further inland than the Sultan's dominions. The Sultan replied that his sphere of influence extended so far inland as to include all the territory in question; that the chiefs who had made the treaties were his subjects; and that as he had not sanctioned the treaties they were null and void.

British influence in Zanzibar was at this time all-powerful, owing to the consummate tact of our Consul-General, Sir John Kirk. His influence over the Sultan was supreme, and he was able to induce Said Barghash to accept a compromise, which secured a peaceful escape from an awkward position. The Sultan's claims were indefinite; and it was not clear to how much territory he had a just title. He was persuaded to allow his boundaries to be defined by an international agreement. After a commission of inquiry, it was agreed that the dominions of the Sultan were Zanzibar, Pemba, the Lamu archipelago, and some smaller islands; in addition to a ten mile belt along the coast from Tunghi Bay to Kipini at the mouth of the Ozi, and the ports of Kismayu, Brava, Merka and Magadoxo, with the land for ten miles around each of them. The territory behind the Sultan's ten-mile slip was divided into two parts; the southern portion was declared to be under the influence of Germany, and the northern was assigned to England.

This agreement was accepted in 1886, and early in

ZANZIBAR NATIVES: GATHERING CLOVES

THE BRITISH EAST AFRICA COMPANY

1887 the Sultan of Zanzibar granted a concession of all his territory on the mainland, that lay in front of the British sphere of influence, to the British East African Association. Said Barghash had offered a concession of the whole of his mainland territories to a British syndicate, but the offer was rejected at the instance of the British Government. But this limited concession was now officially approved, and it was granted on 25th May, 1887. The Association in the following year was reconstituted as the British East Africa Company, which received a Royal Charter on 3rd September, 1888.

In March, 1888, the great Said Barghash died. He was succeeded by Said Khalifa, who, in April, 1888, granted a concession of the district that fronted the German sphere to a German East African Company. The terms of the concession were practically identical with those under which the British East Africa Company held its territories. The German forces arrived to take possession in August.

The annexation was necessarily unpopular among the leading natives, but probably there would have been no serious opposition to the change of government but for an unlucky accident. The German Governor of Pangani had taken with him some dogs. The day he landed, one of these wretched poodles strayed into a mosque; the Governor rushed in to take the dog away, knowing how outraged the

Mohammedans would be by this most unholy profanation of their mosque. This action was misunderstood or misrepresented. The news spread through the town that the Governor had marched into the mosque with his dogs; the population rose *en masse*, and the Governor was expelled.

Mr. George S. Mackenzie arrived at Mombasa to undertake the administration of British East Africa at about the same time. He also was received with suspicion; but by the presence of two British men-of-war and of some of the Sultan of Zanzibar's troops order was maintained.

Mr. Mackenzie, with sound judgment, allowed the Sultan's flag to be retained, and the Arab Lewali to keep their appointments as governors of the coast towns. Thus the native suspicions were allayed, and the Company peacefully initiated its rule in its capital, the historic city of Mombasa.

The administrator of the British East Africa Company, immediately on his arrival, was faced by two difficulties, for neither of which was the Company responsible. These were the insurrections in German East Africa, and the injudicious actions of the British missionaries in the stations near Mombasa.

At this time the British Government—possibly owing to its reliance on German help in Egypt—was behaving with great consideration to the German Colonial party. The Germans found it necessary to

THE BRITISH EAST AFRICA COMPANY 131

blockade the coast of German East Africa to enable them to suppress the rebellion there. It was manifestly useless to blockade the southern coast so long as free trade was allowed immediately to the north. So, to help Germany, the English Government agreed to blockade its own coast and stop the trade of its own subjects. The blockade, of course, was bitterly resented by the native traders, who objected to their trade being stopped in order to punish the subjects of an adjacent country.

The east coast Arabs were also aggrieved by the action of missionaries, who systematically used their stations as asylums for runaway slaves. This question placed the Company's administrator in a very uncomfortable dilemma. The British East Africa Company's motto was "Light and Liberty." As the administrator of a Company with such ideals, Mr. Mackenzie was most reluctant, as his first important official act, to consign again to slavery a number of refugees, some of whom had been for years resident on the mission stations. On the other hand, to have admitted the missionaries' right to harbour fugitive slaves would have been fatal to the industrial system of British East Africa, and would have alienated the Arab support. Sudden interference with the labour system, on which all the coast plantations were cultivated, would have meant the commercial ruin of the coastlands, and immediate Arab rebellion. The policy would have been suicidal. Mackenzie accordingly decided to persuade the Arabs to grant their freedom to all the escaped slaves, then resident at the mission stations, on payment of a moderate compensation. The Arabs agreed to this arrangement, while the missionaries promised not to give asylum to any future refugees. On 1st January, 1889, the escaped slaves were assembled at Rabai, and by the payment of £3,500 compensation, the British East Africa Company generously secured the freedom of 1,422 slaves.

The Company's officers by this action gained the goodwill of the native merchants and planters, on whose prosperity depended the chance of the country being able to pay its way. Mr. Mackenzie worked in sympathetic co-operation with the Lewali of Mombasa, and the future looked propitious. But unfortunately the Company's energies were soon withdrawn from the development of the territory already acquired to a prolonged and ruinous struggle with Germany for the comparatively worthless district of Witu.

The original concession granted to the British East Africa Company by the Sultan, only applied to the territory between the Umba River on the south and the port of Kipini, at the mouth of the Ozi, to the north; the long tract of coast between the Ozi and the Juba, and the islands off the coast, were to be

THE BRITISH EAST AFRICA COMPANY

dealt with by a subsequent agreement. Their cession to the Company, however, had been verbally promised by Said Barghash, and the promise had been confirmed by his successor. The German agreement with England in 1886 defined the southern limit of British East Africa, and across that frontier line the Germans guaranteed not to encroach. There was not, however, in the Anglo-German agreement any explicit clause restricting the Germans from operating in the territory north of the Tana River, which river the agreement defined as the northern boundary of the British sphere.

Immediately to the north of the Tana, in the angle between that river and the coast, was the independent state of Witu. It had been founded by a Suahili outlaw, named Fumo Bakari, who had collected a powerful band of Suahili ruffians. Under his control Witu became an East African Cave of Adullam, where escaped criminals and fraudulent bankrupts found safe refuge. Thence these miscreants raided the plantations of the surrounding villagers, and of the peaceful Pokomo along the Tana.

To protect the coast villages from the "Sultan" of Witu a force of 600 men was sent from Zanzibar in 1885; but as some German traders had previously settled in Witu, Bismarck at once protested against this measure as likely to jeopardize their commercial interests. The country was at the same time declared to be a German protectorate. A "Witu Company," with a capital of £25,000, was founded in 1887 to exploit the country, and strong efforts were made to secure a German footing in the island of Lamu, which is the natural port for the Witu district. At the end of 1888 the German Consul-General at Zanzibar made a formal demand for a cession of the island of Lamu. The Sultan refused, and immediately (January, 1889) offered Sir William Mackinnon, as representative of the British East Africa Company, a lease of Lamu and the adjacent islands. The German Government objected to any such cession, and the matter was referred to the arbitration of Baron Lambermont, who was then Foreign Minister to the King of the Belgians. His award dismissed the German claims to Lamu and the other islands of the Lamu archipelago, and affirmed the Sultan of Zanzibar's right to cede them to whomsoever he chose. This award was given in August, 1889, and the Sultan of Zanzibar at once granted a concession of the whole of his territories north of the Tana to the British East Africa Company. As this gave the Company the land between Witu and the coast, the successful administration of Witu by Germany was rendered impossible.

The indomitable Germans had one last try to maintain their position at Witu by connecting it with the coast to the north of Lamu. On 22nd October, 1889, Germany proclaimed a protectorate over the whole of the Sultan

THE BRITISH EAST AFRICA COMPANY 135

of Zanzibar's territory between the Juba and Witu; and later on it maintained that the islands of Manda and Patta, which are situated a little to the north of Lamu, were part of the Witu protectorate, and therefore under German control. The British East Africa Company had already occupied these islands, but the British Government ordered the Company to withdraw its agent and flag until its rights were confirmed. The question was submitted to arbitration. The award affirmed the legality of the concession under which the Company had occupied the islands, and repudiated the German claims. Accordingly, in October, 1890, the Government gave the Company permission to resume occupation.

This award rendered the German occupation of Witu valueless, and the German Witu Company offered to sell its rights and properties to the British Chartered Company. There was no particular reason why the British Company should buy them, and the negotiations were fruitless. So the German agents resolved not to give in without another struggle. Their aim in endeavouring to secure Lamu was to gain the right to levy customs over the trade of the Tana Valley, which finds its outlet through that port. There was, however, another way of taxing the Tana trade. Most of it passes through the Belesoni Canal a small artificial canoe channel which connects the Tana and the Ozi. This interesting canal was built in order to facilitate the trade between Lamu and the Upper Tana. The mouth of the Tana is obstructed by a bar, which renders its navigation difficult; but at a distance (measured in a straight line) of eight miles from the shore, the Tana approaches within two miles of a bend of the Ozi. The estuary of the Ozi is not only about twenty miles nearer Lamu than the mouth of the Tana, but it offers a safe harbour to native dhows.

The whole of the commercial produce of the Tana Valley is carried down in dug-out canoes or "mau," which pass through the Belesoni Canal to Kau and Kipini, the two ports on the Ozi estuary. There goods are transhipped to coasting dhows, which carry their cargoes to Lamu.

It was, therefore, as easy to tax the Tana trade at the Belesoni Canal as at Lamu. The Sultan of Witu accordingly placed a custom house on the Canal, and imposed dues. This act was apparently suggested by the German traders. Supported by them, the Sultan refused to remove the custom house when ordered to do so by the British East Africa Company. The Belesoni Canal was clearly within the territory belonging to Zanzibar; accordingly the Company called on the British Government to protect the territory of our vassal, the Sultan of Zanzibar. The Government not only declined to interfere, but objected to action being taken by the Sultan, as any such course would

THE BRITISH EAST AFRICA COMPANY 137

lead to friction with Germany. The Company accordingly resolved to take action itself. It despatched a body of troops to the district, under Clifford Crauford (late Commissioner at Mombasa), and sent an ultimatum to Witu, demanding the removal of the custom house by December 31st. The German Consul-General advised Fumo Bakari to submit. According to the chief, he had occupied the Canal at the request of the Germans and on a promise of assistance from them; so this advice showed him that he had no chance of armed support, and he was compelled to obey.

Thus step by step Germany's opposition to the extension of the British East Africa Company's sphere of influence was thwarted by the power of the Company's local forces and the overwhelming evidence in favour of the legality of its position. It is impossible, however, to read the tedious correspondence respecting the ownership of these northern coastlands without feeling that the Company, by its insistence, secured for the empire rights which the Government would have allowed to pass to Germany unquestioned.

While this controversy had been going on between the Governments, the jingo section of the German Colonial party had taken a step which was practically an appeal to arms. It despatched an expedition across British East Africa, which, whatever the objects of its founders may have been, was conducted as a piratical raid.

News of this undertaking was first received in October, 1888, when it was stated that Lieutenant Wissmann and Dr. Carl Peters were appointed leaders of an expedition which was to march up the Tana Valley to the Upper Nile, with the object of securing a German route from the eastern coast to Emin's Equatorial Province. The expedition was, nominally, for the relief of Emin Pasha; but after the arrival of the news in January, 1889, that Stanley had rescued Emin, who was on his way back to the coast, the excuse was not taken seriously. Wissmann, having received an appointment in German East Africa, Carl Peters was given the command, and left Berlin in February, 1889. At Aden he enlisted one hundred Somali, who were taken to Bagamoyo, in German East Africa. The German Government refused to allow Peters to pass through German East Africa, and the British squadron endeavoured to prevent his landing on the British coast. But Peters successfully ran the blockade through the British fleet, and landed at Kwyhu Bay on June 15th. He made a long stay at Witu to organize his caravan, and on July 27th started up the Tana Valley. Peters at once displayed his real purpose; a British expedition under Mr. J. R. W. Piggott, who was the first Englishman to explore the Tana Valley, had negotiated treaties with the Tana tribes, and established stations on behalf of the British East Africa Company. Peters tore up the treaties whenever he could find them; he burnt the Company's stations; he pulled down its flag; he attacked the Pokomo, one of the most peaceful tribes in Africa, and compelled them to give him food for nothing. He left behind him a trail of blood and desolation, for which later travellers had to suffer.

As soon as the British East Africa Company's administrator heard that Peters had effected a landing, he sent an expedition to the Tana Valley to stop him. The expedition was under the command of a young shipping clerk, who was a man of much literary ability, but who—to put it mildly—was not a soldier. He felt that his force was too weak to compel the reckless Peters to return, and so allowed him to proceed unmolested. He followed the German expedition, watching it from a respectful distance, until his caravan stumbled across a raiding party of Somali, from whom most of the men fled in dismay. A half-caste Arab rallied a few of the Zanzibari escort, and defended the stores of the caravan against the Somali with such courage that the robbers were driven off, but at the cost of the life of the faithful Arab. After this incident, the caravan was too disorganized to be of any use as a check to Peters, and it returned to Mombasa. There the survivors of the gallant men, who defeated the Somali and saved the caravan, were sentenced to a severe flogging, from which, however, they were saved by an inquiry.

The collapse of the British expedition left Peters free to continue his march unchecked. He displayed magnificent courage and great military skill. The difficulties in his way were serious, but he forced his way through them all. He marched nearly the whole length of the Tana Valley, and then across the Kikuyu country on to the plains of Laikipia. There he was opposed by the Masai, but in two hard-fought battles the accurate fire of the Somali escort broke the Masai charge. As the prize of victory, Peters secured big herds of cattle, which supplied his caravan with abundant food. He descended to Baringo, hoisted the German flag at Njemps, ravaged Kamasia and entered Uganda. All along his route Peters had annexed the country in the name of the German Empire. In Uganda he negotiated a treaty with Mwanga, in the interests of Germany (*vide* p. 172), and then hastened home by the western side of the Victoria Nyanza.

On his return to the coast, however, he found that his labours were all in vain. A treaty had been signed between England and Germany, by which the latter withdrew her protectorates over Witu and the territory to the north of the Tana, on the understanding that England should secure for Germany the definite cession of the territories held in lease from the Sultan of Zanzibar, and in exchange for the retrocession of Heligoland.

This treaty of 1st July, 1890, closed the long struggle

THE BRITISH EAST AFRICA COMPANY 141

with Germany in East Africa. It left the British East Africa Company in undisputed possession of the whole of the vast region between the frontier of British East Africa on the south, and the Juba River and Abyssinia on the north. The Company was fairly entitled to this territory, which, apart from its action, Germany would have been allowed to annex without serious protest.

But the territory soon proved a useless and expensive encumbrance, and troubles began at once.

The Sultan of Witu had granted a timber concession to a German syndicate, and in August, 1890, a party of eleven Germans landed at Lamu to work it. The Sultan considered that the Germans had led him into conflict with the British, and had left him in the lurch when trouble came; he was, therefore, very angry with his former allies. The timber workers were warned at Lamu against going to Witu; but their leader, Kuntzel, who had once been on very friendly terms with the Sultan, was confident that there was no danger. The party arrived in Witu on September 14th, and there was a stormy interview between the Sultan and Kuntzel. The latter saw that it was useless to attempt working the concession at present, and decided to return to the coast. The gatekeeper refused to let the Germans out of the town, and Kuntzel, fearing treachery, shot the man and endeavoured to force the gate. The whole party was at once surrounded; the Germans fought with magnificent courage, but the odds were overwhelming, and only one man escaped to tell the story.

The German Government called on England to avenge the massacre, and a naval brigade under Admiral Sir E. Freemantle marched against Witu. The Sultan assured his troops that Englishmen could only fight at sea, and under this impression the naval brigade was attacked on the march, when the Witu army was easily routed. The brigade forced its way to an old Galla village on a hill to the south of the town, and bombarded it. A war rocket set fire to the huts, and the whole town, including the Sultan's palace, was soon in flames. The rebels evacuated the place and withdrew into the forests to the north, whence they have long continued to harass the country and defy the British authorities.

To hold Witu against the rebels, the town was occupied by a company of Indian troops, and connected with the coast by a road and a telephone. The garrison easily maintained the place against the natives; but, economically, the country has been a disappointment. The climate is deadly; the trade dwindled to insignificance; the coffee and cotton plantations were a failure, and the expense of maintaining the Indian contingent was too heavy for the British East Africa Company to continue in a country which gave such poor promise of commercial success. After the angry quarrel for its possession, and the

THE BRITISH EAST AFRICA COMPANY 143

sacrifices made for it, Witu proved a white elephant which the Company could not afford to feed. So in 1893 it announced its intention of withdrawing its garrison and abandoning the country. The Imperial Government had given Heligoland to Germany in return for Witu, and after this sacrifice the country could not be allowed to go derelict. The Government could not prevent the Company's withdrawal; so to save the friendly natives from the revenge of the outlaws, and the loss of the main compensation received for Heligoland, the Government took over the administration of the Witu province.

Chapter IX

THE MAZRUI REBELLION AND EMIGRATION

"Vita havina mato."
"War has no eyes."
—*Zanzibari Proverb.*

THE leading family of the East African Arabs is that known as the Mazrui or Mazaria. According to one account of their origin, the Mazrui are descended from an Arab named Abdulla, who emigrated from Oman, the south-eastern province of Arabia, and settled in Mombasa at the end of the seventeenth century. According to another story, the clan is of much greater antiquity, and is descended from some Arabs who settled on the coast before the advent of the Portuguese. Whichever theory be true, the Mazrui have been the leaders of the east coast Arabs for at least the last two centuries.

Early in the eighteenth century a Mazrui chief Mahommad-bin-Othman, was appointed Lewali of Mombasa, and his descendants ruled the coast as the representatives of the Iman of Oman until 1750. A

MAZRUI REBELLION AND EMIGRATION 145

political change then occurred in Oman, and the Yorabi dynasty was succeeded by that of the Albusaidi. The Mazrui refused to acknowledge the new dynasty, and led a revolt of the east coast Arabs against Oman. The movement was successful, and successive heads of the Mazrui family ruled Mombasa as independent Sultans. In 1806, on the accession of Said Said, the fourth member of the Albusaidi dynasty, the first serious attempt was made by Oman to reconquer its former East African possessions. A long war ensued, in which the Muscat Arabs gradually gained ground. They defeated the Mazrui, reconquered the east coast islands, and prepared to attack Mombasa. At this juncture two British men-of-war, which were engaged in the Admiralty survey of the coast, entered the harbour.

Suliman, the Sultan of Mombasa, appealed to the British for help, and a treaty was negotiated, by which the town was placed under British protection. This secured the Mazrui a respite. Captain Vidal's action was, however, repudiated by the British Government, which had no wish to interfere between the friendly state of Oman and its revolted subjects. The treaty was not ratified, and the English flag withdrawn.

Mombasa was thus abandoned to the tender mercies of the Muscat Arabs. It made a stubborn defence, and capitulated on terms in 1826; twice, however, it revolted, and was recaptured. It finally fell in 1837

The Sultan Rashid surrendered on conditions which were immediately disregarded, and he, the last independent Sultan of Mombasa, with several of his principal supporters, was left to die of starvation in a dungeon on the Persian Gulf.

The general rank and file of the Mazrui were punished by expulsion from Mombasa. One party, under Rashid's brother Abdulla, went south to Gazi, a port on the coast about thirty miles from Mombasa. Another branch of the clan settled at Takaungu, a small town beside the estuary of the Khilifi, thirty miles north of Mombasa. Both parties formed semi-independent states, though they were nominally subject to the Sultan of Zanzibar.

Rashid's son, Mbaruk, had been taken south by his uncle in the flight from Mombasa, and on succeeding Abdulla as head of the Gazi Mazrui, he resolved to recover the complete independence of the coast. To secure the unity of the whole Mazrui clan in the fight for "Home Rule," he attempted in 1865 to conquer the section settled at Takaungu. This attack was defeated, owing to the help given to the defenders by Said Said, the Sultan of Zanzibar, who now, owing to Lord Canning's award was suzerain of the East African coastlands.

Mbaruk retreated sullenly to Gazi. On his way south he called at the mission station at Ribe, where he saw New. Apparently he intended mischief, as he

MOMBASA.

By kind permission of Sir John Kirk, G.C.M.G.

MAZRUI REBELLION AND EMIGRATION 147

declined to accept New's hospitality; and it is stated that he shortly afterwards formed a plot to capture the missionaries, who took shelter in Mombasa until the danger was past. Mbaruk then thrice rebelled against Zanzibar. He was defeated, and his chief stronghold Mwele was captured after an eighteen days' siege. But the irrepressible Mbaruk escaped to the bush, and after the return of the Zanzibar forces he avenged the invasion of his country by looting Mombasa.

In his old age, however, Mbaruk of Gazi had settled down to a peaceful life. He lived at Gazi, and ruled the province as the vassal to the Sultan of Zanzibar. On the establishment of the British East Africa Company, he gave its representative a cordial welcome and invaluable support, and there can be no doubt that his highest ambition was to spend the rest of his days at ease and in peace.

But circumstances were too strong for him, and he was reluctantly driven to head a formidable rising against British rule, and finally to lead an exodus from British territory.

We have already seen that the Company's first administrator, Mr. George S. Mackenzie, had to face a strong prejudice against European rule, owing partly to sympathy with the national insurrection in German East Africa, and partly due to an old quarrel with the missionaries. Mackenzie, however, conquered this prejudice by tact, and a sympathetic appreciation of the natives' view of British policy.

But in the latter period of the British East Africa Company's administration its rule caused great local dissatisfaction. The first cause of this dissatisfaction was the conflict between the natives and the missionaries.

Krapf's Mission in East Africa had been warmly welcomed by Said Said, who was then the Sultan of Zanzibar, and the local authorities. It was felt that the aim of the missionaries was to convert the heathen to a religion which had many points in common with Islam. The Sultan gave the missions land for schools and stations. But after the establishment of the British East Africa Company's rule, the Church Missionary Society's agents at Mombasa devoted their energies mainly to proselytism among the Mohammedans. This action was not surprising, for the cultured, educated Mohammedans could better understand the truths of Christianity than the fetish-worshipping Wanyika.

As the missionaries were on very intimate terms with the officials of the British East Africa Company—one of the Company's administrators, for example, served as the Missionary Society's Treasurer—the Company was regarded as partly responsible for this anti-Islam movement.

A second factor which led to dissatisfaction with the Company's rule was interference with slavery

MAZRUI REBELLION AND EMIGRATION 149

though for this the Company itself was certainly not to blame. Almost immediately after the establishment of the Company in Mombasa, under pressure from the British Government, the Sultan of Zanzibar, Said Khalifa, issued a decree proclaiming the freedom of all slaves who entered his territory overland. This law was followed by another enacted by his successor, Said Ali, who prohibited the sale of slaves altogether. The latter decree was at first kept secret on the mainland by the Company's administrator, who certainly acted, or allowed his subordinates to act, in defiance of it.

But however strongly the Company's local agents were opposed to the measure, and however ingeniously they tried to evade it, they could not help ultimately obeying it in the towns under their immediate observance. Hence in Mombasa, Lamu, and Melindi, the new decrees were at length enforced, with disastrous consequences to the industrial system of the coast. In addition to the economic consequences of its disturbance to trade, it did even more harm by the blow it struck at the British reputation for justice. Sir Arthur Hardinge, in the course of a judicial and masterly summary of the causes of the Mazrui rebellion, clearly expresses the shock to native opinion of this unfortunate interference. " To the native, to whom the European objections to slavery and slave-dealing appear as fantastic and unintelligible as do the socialistic protests against private property to the ordinary Englishman, this upsetting of all the old arrangements sanctioned for centuries by religion and native public opinion seemed an act of gratuitous oppression, and shook the confidence which other circumstances, such as the surprising integrity and patience of our magistrates, had encouraged in the justice of British rule."

For these, and some less important reasons, the Company's rule was unpopular with the coast Arabs. But the peace was kept, for it was well known along the coast that the Company was in serious difficulties, that its days were numbered, and that the coast would shortly be again ruled from Zanzibar. A conflict, however, broke out over the chieftainship of Takaungu in the spring of 1895.

The Takaungu branch of the Mazrui had been founded by Hamis, the head of the younger branch of the clan. Since its establishment after the expulsion from Mombasa in 1837, and throughout the period of Mbaruk of Gazi's long conflict with Zanzibar, the Takaungu Mazrui had been quietly growing in power and numbers. Hamis was succeeded by his brother Said, who was followed by Rashid and Salim, two sons of Hamis. On Salim's death in February, 1895, his nephew Mbaruk was the rightful heir to the chieftainship.[1] But the British East Africa Company appointed the wrongful heir, Salim's son Rashid, owing

---

[1] The relationships of the heads of the Takaungu clan are shown in the following table :—

MAZRUI REBELLION AND EMIGRATION

to his greater friendliness to the British. Mbaruk, the son of Rashid, who, to distinguish him from the chief of Gazi, is usually known as Mbaruk of Takaungu, appeared to submit to the decision. He settled at Gonjoro, and there quietly obtained control of the 1,200 armed retainers of the late chief. A crisis resulted from a personal quarrel between the rightful chief and the Company's nominee in the street of Takaungu. Mbaruk withdrew to Gonjoro, and threatened armed resistance. The Company's puppet had no following of any importance, and he appealed for help to England. A man-of-war was sent to the harbour of Khilifi, three miles north of Takaungu, and Sir A. Hardinge accompanied it in the hope that he might arrange matters peaceably. As his influence with the Arabs is great, the dispute might have been settled but for an accident. Hardinge went to Gonjoro with a small escort of Zanzibari and men from the warship. Gonjoro was found to be deserted, and Mbaruk was in camp on the adjacent hills. One of the natives was sent to the British camp, where he was challenged by

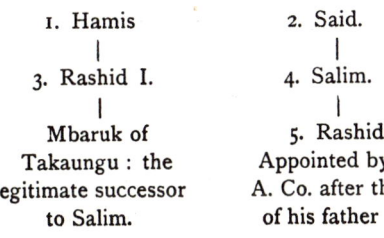

1. Hamis
   |
3. Rashid I.
   |
Mbaruk of Takaungu : the legitimate successor to Salim.

2. Said.
   |
4. Salim.
   |
5. Rashid II. Appointed by B. E. A. Co. after the death of his father Salim.

the sentries, who tried to stop him. A gun went off in the scuffle; Mbaruk's men thought their envoy had been treacherously shot, and immediately opened fire.

Owing to this misunderstanding, the disastrous Mazrui rebellion was begun. Mbaruk was easily defeated at Gonjoro, and fled to Sokoki, a village in the forests to the north. His brother Aziz immediately attacked Tanganyika, a neighbouring trading settlement, inhabited by many Indian merchants, and looted the bazaar. Aziz was expelled by a force of Zanzibari, and Sir Lloyd Matthews pursued Mbaruk, who was soon expelled from Sokoki. He fled south, and took refuge with his kinsman Mbaruk of Gazi.

It was while affairs were in this disturbed condition that the rule of the British East Africa Company came to an end. The Company had failed to make the country pay working expenses, or offer any hope that it would do so in the near future, and it was, therefore, obliged to resign its charter. The causes of the Company's failure were manifold, but the chief factor was an absorption in political and philanthropic schemes, which necessitated an expensive administration, and was accompanied by neglect of the economic development of the country. The career of the Company had been disinterested and honourable, but its ideals were impracticable with the resources at its disposal. Its high motives were forgotten in the obloquy of failure, and its end was marked by unmerited insult and contempt.

MAZRUI REBELLION AND EMIGRATION 153

The transfer of the administration from the Company to the Imperial Government was completed at Mombasa on 8th and 9th July, 1895. Sir Arthur Hardinge landed to take charge of the country on behalf of the Foreign Office, and he was immediately confronted by the dispute over the chieftainship of Takaungu.

He at once warned Mbaruk of Gazi that Mbaruk of Takaungu was a rebel, and asked for his surrender. Mbaruk of Gazi came in person, professed the utmost loyalty, and begged for time. Sir Arthur Hardinge's demand had placed Mbaruk of Gazi in a very awkward position. He had no particular reason for gratitude either to England or to Zanzibar. His father had been abandoned by England to the Muscat Arabs, and, in consequence, died a horrible and treacherous death. The rule of the British East Africa Company had been accompanied by an interference with slavery, which had wrought the commercial ruin of the coast plantations. Nevertheless, Mbaruk had loyally supported the Company; he had helped to suppress a rebellion at Mombasa, to crush a rising in Taita, and to protect the Tana missions against the Witu rebels. His interests now were all on the side of peace. He was an old man, his father having died in 1837. He had a subsidy from the Government of 1900 rupees a month for the administration of his district; and his own residence on the coast at Gazi, where he lived in dignity and comfort, was at the mercy of the British gun-boats. He had the alternatives of surrendering his kinsman, and living his last days in comfort and dignity as the prince of the south-eastern corner of British East Africa; or of refusing the demand, in which case his highest possible position was that of an outlaw chief, in the back bush of the coastlands and in the Nyika.

He knew, however, that Mbaruk of Takaungu had been driven to rebellion by an act of injustice, and he was bound to his cousin both by blood and the Arab obligations of hospitality. So a direct obedience to the British demand seemed to him dishonourable. He wrote a pathetic appeal for peace.

"I do not want war against the Government at all. I want peace for myself and all my people, and my son Mbaruk. If anything happens I am responsible. . . . If you do not want to give me peace, I want permission to send a telegram and to wait for the reply. I will abide by any reply I receive. This is what I want from you. I want peace from the Government, and this is not a great thing for them to do, and to give me the time for a reply from England. Alla, halla; alla, halla. I want peace; I do not want war with the Government. I am not able at all to fight. I have never done this when I was in the Company's service, and now also I cannot do it. I want to be just like before. Do not you drive me to make trouble with the Government. Alla, halla; alla, halla. This is what I want from you.

MAZRUI REBELLION AND EMIGRATION 155

The rest is for you. I will obey the order. Give my salaams to General Matthews, the Admiral, and Mr. Piggott.

(Signed) "MBARUK-BIN-RASHID."

A week after Mbaruk's visit to Mombasa the fighting broke out again. Aziz, a brother of Mbaruk of Takaungu, had vowed not to shave until he had avenged his brother's wrongs. He quietly collected men, and suddenly attacked Takaungu. He forced his way into the town, and seized the mosque. Thence he attacked the cantonments, which were occupied by a force of Zanzibari under Captain Raikes. The garrison made a gallant resistance, repelled the attack, and captured the mosque. The rebels were finally driven from the town, but not until they had looted and burnt most of it. Aziz withdrew to Sokoki, whence he was driven by a naval brigade. He then fled south to join his brother at Gazi.

After this renewal of rebellion Mbaruk of Gazi offered to allow the authorities to seize the rebel chiefs, but refused himself to take any part in the proceedings. Sir Arthur Hardinge and a powerful force left Mombasa to effect the arrests. The expedition arrived too late; the rebels had heard of its approach and fled to Mwele, a stronghold some three days' march inland. As the naval brigade approached, Mbaruk of Gazi was persuaded to throw in his lot with the rebels. He abandoned Gazi, and retreated to Mwele. The port of Wanga was immediately attacked by the natives, and the bazaars looted.

An ultimatum was then sent to Mbaruk, demanding the surrender of the rebel chiefs within a fortnight. At the end of this time a naval brigade, under Admiral Rawson, marched inland to Mwele, which was taken, after what the official despatch describes as "two hours' hard fighting."

Mbaruk of Takaungu and Aziz fled at the beginning of the fight; but the gallant old Mbaruk of Gazi only escaped after the British had entered the boma, and Zahran-bin-Rashid, the commander of his forces, had been shot through the head by a Soudanese at the main gate.

Mbaruk withdrew into the bush, and for the rest of 1895 maintained a guerilla warfare, which caused confusion through the whole country, from Melindi on the north to the German frontier on the south.

At first the rebels scored some considerable successes. On the 16th October, in an attack on a stockade at Mgobani, near Gazi, Captain Lawrence was killed and his force scattered. A month later the rebels attacked Mazeras, a station ten miles from Mombasa, where the British East Africa Company had begun a small silver-lead mine. They also attacked Rabai, and captured a camel caravan, which was under an escort of Beluchi, on the Uganda Road; they killed the jemadar in command,

MAZRUI REBELLION AND EMIGRATION 157

but for some reason they only carried away 20 out of the 700 loads captured.

The rebellion was at first confined to the Mazrui chiefs. But their success soon gained for the rebels adherents among the Suahili chiefs and the native tribes who had kept aloof at first, as the quarrel was over an infringement of the Arab rules of succession. The country between Mombasa and Takaungu is under the influence of a Suahili chief, whose principal town is on the Mtwapa river, seven miles north of Mombasa. The chief was believed to be secretly aiding the Mazrui, and he was summoned to Mombasa to answer for his conduct. Though he was an old man, eighty years of age, he declined to obey, and openly joined the rebels.

This was the signal for a general rising of the East Coast natives, and practically the whole of the British East African coast lands were in rebellion, and the British power confined to the coast ports.

The situation was now very serious, as it had quite outgrown the power of the local forces. The naval brigade could carry any position it attacked, but its movements were necessarily slow. It could not follow up a success, so as to inflict serious loss upon the rebels, and it could not defend friendly villages from attack. An Indian contingent was therefore called for. Three hundred men, under Captain Barrett and Lieutenant Scott, landed on 30th December, 1895. The first duty of the Indian contingent was to clear the immediate neighbourhood of Mombasa. A fortnight after its arrival it attacked Mtwapa. The landing was steadily resisted, and there was a three hours' engagement between the boats and the natives on shore. The rebel casualties numbered eighteen, and two of the attacking force were wounded. The rebels then withdrew to a boma, some miles to the north. The Indian troops followed in pursuit next day. The column was purposely misled by the guides; it marched for twenty-two hours across waterless country, and finally arrived at a village on the shore, where all the wells had been filled in. Luckily, near the village there is a cocoa-nut plantation, which saved the force from disaster. The milk of the nuts staved off thirst starvation until water could be found. The pursuit was abandoned, and the contingent returned directly to Mombasa.

The rebels followed the retreating column, and on 21st January actually attacked Freretown; but, owing to the defence of the Indian and Soudanese troops, the attack was repelled.

A second expedition against the rebel boma to the north was then organized. It was successfully accomplished, and a small garrison, under a sepoy officer, established in the district. The safety of Mombasa and its adjacent mission stations was thus secured.

Two columns were then organized to march through the country and disperse the rebels. The northern column was sent out to drive the rebels southward, and

MAZRUI REBELLION AND EMIGRATION 159

prevent the rebellion spreading among the northern coast tribes. The rebels, however, succeeded in eluding the column, and, while it was working south, they fell on Melindi, burnt 400 houses in the town, looted some Indian shops, and killed several people.

This success broke the confidence of the Giriama, the most powerful tribe on the coast of British East Africa. They had previously held aloof from rebellion, but now made a demonstration against the village of Sandia. Had they done more the consequences would have been disastrous. But Sir A. Hardinge held a conference with the Giriama elders, and they swore fidelity on their sacred animal, the hyena.

The southern column had meanwhile been operating against Mbaruk, and chasing him from post to post. His country was devastated, and his chief villages destroyed. But his forces were not seriously injured, and, as soon as the column began its return march to the coast, they harassed the rearguard. The southern column then invaded Shimba, a hilly country south of Mombasa. A station was established, and an Indian garrison left under the command of Lieutenant Scott. Although the rebels had been twice defeated (2nd and 6th of March), no sooner had the main force returned to Mombasa than the post was attacked.

The Shimba expedition was undertaken at the beginning of March, and it showed that the forces available were still insufficient to cope with the rebellion.

The civil authorities had already realized this fact, and an Indian regiment was on the way to Mombasa. It landed on March 15th, and its commander, Colonel Pearson, at once began a systematic campaign to separate the different rebel centres, and crush them in detail. His plan of campaign was to establish a chain of forts westward from Mombasa along the Uganda Road, and another chain along the southern frontier. So soon as these stations were fairly established, Colonel Pearson advanced to attack Mbaruk's main force, which was assembled in the Kamari Forest, and to clear the whole country between the Uganda Road and the German frontier. On April 4th the columns were ready to storm Mweni, a village in the Kamari Forest. The advance was begun at 2 a.m., the village was reached before dawn, and triumphantly carried by storm. Its garrison was found to consist of one cripple, an old woman. This battle was typical of the rest. Colonel Pearson's force was too powerful for any opposition to be offered; he sent out numerous divisions, which scoured the country, chasing the rebels from village to village, and destroying the plantations. At length Mbaruk saw the struggle was hopeless. So he and his men crossed the frontier into German territory. They at once surrendered (April 20th) to Major von Wissmann, who gladly received the refugees and settled them in Usaramo, a fertile but then uninhabited district.

FORT MOMBASA.

MAZRUI REBELLION AND EMIGRATION

By the end of April the Mazrui rebellion was thus at an end. But the victory was gained at the cost of wholesale devastation and disorganization. The greatest loss, however, was the emigration of the most intelligent and profitable section of the East Coast natives, a heavy price in a country whose main need is population.

A village elder was asked whether his people had suffered much by the war. "Alas!" he replied, "when two elephants meet in conflict, what becomes of the grass beneath their feet?"

Chapter X

HOW THE MISSIONARIES RETURNED TO UGANDA

"Watu waliambiwa 'Kakaeni'; hawa kuambiwa 'Kashindaneni.'"
"People were told 'Go and dwell'; they were not told 'Go and struggle together for the mastery.'"
—*Suahili Proverb* (*W. E. Taylor*).

IT is now time to turn from the coast lands to the progress of events in the interior. We have seen in a previous chapter what keen interest in the hinterland was aroused by Stanley's appeal for missionaries to Uganda, and how, in response to that appeal, parties of Protestant and Catholic missionaries entered the country. By their quarrels they lost Mtesa's confidence, and the missions made no effective progress during his lifetime.

Mtesa died in 1884, and his successor, Mwanga, being bound by no pledges to the missions, prepared to suppress them. He began fitfully to persecute the native converts, and to harass the missionaries. Mwanga's murder of Bishop Hannington, who was approaching Uganda by a road which native superstition closed to Europeans, led to more active measures against the missionaries. Their position became so precarious that they all withdrew and established stations at the southern end of the Victoria Nyanza, to await a more favourable opportunity for work in Uganda.

In 1888 Mwanga prepared for a general massacre of all his Christian and Mohammedan subjects. They were to be deported to an uninhabited island, and there left to starve. The primitive paganism was to be re-established as the universal religion of Uganda. News of the project leaked out. The two threatened parties joined forces. They rebelled suddenly and successfully. Mwanga fled, and his brother, Kiwewa, was proclaimed king in his stead. The victors promptly quarrelled over the division of the spoil. The Christians were the weaker party, so they fled to the province of Ankori; and Kiwewa reigned as the nominee of the Mohammedans. He quarrelled with his supporters, and, in a fit of rage, killed the Mohammedan leader, Mujasi, with his own hands. In revenge for this murder the Mohammedans stormed the palace. Kiwewa escaped to the tomb of his father Mtesa, but he was denied sanctuary there, and fled from Uganda. The Mohammedans then placed upon the throne Kalema (or Karema), a third son of Mtesa.

While these events were happening in Uganda, Mwanga had not been idle. He had taken refuge in the French mission station at Bukumbi, on the southern side of the lake. He professed repentance of his sins, and conversion to the Roman Catholic faith. He was forgiven by the Fathers, and instigated by them to attempt the recovery of his throne. The Protestant missionaries, distrusting Mwanga's sincerity, and fearing that his murder of their Bishop would permanently estrange him from their side, either strongly opposed the scheme or remained neutral. The native Protestants, however, rallied to Mwanga, and joined in a general appeal to him to return.

Mwanga's main difficulty was his poverty in arms and ammunition. The supplies he had previously collected were all in the hands of his foes. The importation of war material into Equatorial Africa for sale to natives was forbidden by the Berlin Act; and at that time this regulation was being rigorously enforced by both the Germans and the British.

Without weapons nothing could be done. So Mwanga and his allies called to their aid an ex-missionary of the name of Stokes. This famous trader played such an important part in the struggle for Uganda that some notice of him is necessary. Stokes was a man who had an exceptionally interesting career. He went to East Africa on the staff of the Church Missionary Society, and he was sent inland to the country of the Wanyamwezi. He was an industrious man, and undertook trading as well as his official work. To strengthen his influence among the tribe, he entered into a domestic alliance with the daughter of a leading Mnyamwezi chief. His trade prospered. His methods were astute, and white ivory was not the only product in which he is said to have dealt. Stokes' English wife died, and he subsequently took his Mnyamwezi concubine to Zanzibar, and there formally married her. This proceeding was against the rules of the Church Missionary Society. According to Mr. Inderwick, who appeared as counsel for that Society in some subsequent proceedings in the Probate Court, since Stokes' marriage with a heathen woman was deemed inconsistent with his position as a missionary, his connection with the Missionary Society came to an end. The Church Missionary Society was probably glad of an excuse to dismiss Stokes; but the devil must have smiled, when Stokes was expelled from the missionary service for the most honourable incident in his record.

Stokes continued trading, and one of his enterprises was his alliance with Mwanga and the French priests for the invasion of Uganda in 1889. His subsequent career may be briefly related. As Unyamwezi was included in German East Africa, Stokes took service as an officer of the German Government. In

1894 he started with a caravan of 1,000 armed men to found a station in the country to the north-west of German East Africa. He suggested to the British authorities that he should be allowed to capture Wadelai; but his offer was emphatically rejected. Sir Henry Colvile, who was then the Administrator of British East Africa, informed Stokes by letter (June, 1894) that he regarded those "1,000 armed men with uneasiness," and remarked, "I wish to warn you that I can only treat any unauthorized warlike operations as acts of piracy."

Stokes halted on the British frontier, where he had an acrimonious correspondence with the British officer instructed to watch his proceedings. The officer told Stokes that he could not "entertain any negotiations with a large armed force, which has looted and murdered in British territory." He therefore abandoned the idea of entering British East Africa, and marched into the Congo Free State. He went westward to join his ally, Hamadi-ben-Ali, better known as Kibonge, who had murdered Emin Pasha, and was then in rebellion against the Free State. Stokes wrote to him, "My dear Kibonge, send me an intelligent messenger, and one who is well acquainted with the truth. I can help. Do not be afraid of being killed. You shall not die. If you have need of me, send me a messenger quickly, and I will immediately come to you." Kibonge's reply, appealing to Stokes for immediate

THE MISSIONARIES RETURN TO UGANDA

help against the Belgians, came too late. Kibonge was captured and hung for the murder of Emin Pasha. Stokes, hastening to Kibonge's aid with a small advanced party, was arrested by Captain Henry. In his possession were found the piracy threat of Sir Henry Colvile, and letters proving both Stokes' complicity in the Arab Congo rebellion and his trade in arms with the rebels. Stokes was court-martialled and hung at Lindi by Major Lothaire, on 15th January, 1895.

Lothaire's conduct of the trial was irregular, as it included several technical errors. The most serious was the inconsistency that Stokes had been refused right of appeal as a soldier, and then was hung instead of being shot. Lothaire was accordingly tried for murder at Boma and acquitted. Captain Arthur, the British representative at the trial, in his official report concluded that Lothaire had "displayed undue haste and precipitation in the trial and execution of Mr. Stokes," but that Lothaire was "rightfully acquitted."

After this brief sketch of Stokes' career, it will be understood that Mwanga could not have applied to a more suitable agent. Stokes was the leading expert in the illicit gunpowder trade, and with his cosmopolitan sympathies was equally ready to help English, Germans, French, Waganda, and Arabs. He undertook, according to his own account, in return for between seventeen and eighteen tons of ivory (worth more than £20,000), to supply Mwanga and the French party with the necessary arms and ammunition. The time seemed favourable for the attempt, as Kalema's rule was unpopular in Uganda. Kalema had heard of the projected invasion, and of a plot in the capital for his deposition; and, as it is the rule in Uganda that the king must be a member of the hereditary royal family, Kalema did his best to render himself indispensable by a massacre of his relatives. Then he slew the old Katikiro, whom Emin had described as "the one gentleman in Uganda" who, through all the religious changes in his country, had remained a firm adherent of the national paganism.

These savage acts horrified many of Kalema's supporters, and facilitated the return of the exiled king. Mwanga sailed from Bukumbi in Stokes' boat, landed at the mouth of the Kagera River, and raised the standard of civil war. He was defeated, and fled to the Sesse Islands, where he was welcomed by the inhabitants. As their canoes were supreme on the lake, Mwanga was safe. With the aid of the Wa-Sesse Mwanga captured Bulingugwe, a small island seven miles from Rubaga, the capital of Uganda. A further attempt on the mainland, though temporarily successful, ultimately failed. Stokes was sent down to the coast for more arms and ammunition, while Mwanga maintained his position at Bulingugwe. Here the king was joined by some of the English missionaries, and members of both missions endeavoured to gain European assistance for Mwanga.

With the irony of fate, which in East African history is especially malicious, both parties invited into Uganda the force to which ultimately it was most bitterly opposed. Mackay appealed to Emin to bring in the Soudanese, the very step for which later on the Protestants so bitterly denounced Lugard. The Catholics, with Mwanga's authority, did their best to persuade the British East Africa Company to occupy Uganda. One of the Company's exploring caravans, under Mr. F. J. Jackson, during the summer of 1889 reached the eastern coast of the Nyanza. Père Lourdel wrote to Mr. Jackson to say that Mwanga "offers you, in addition to the monopoly of commerce in Uganda, a present of one hundred frasila of ivory, which he will give you when he is returned to the throne. He also takes upon himself the provisioning of your men, and accepts your flag. For our part, we Catholic missionaries shall be very glad and very grateful to take advantage of the protection which you will be able, I hope, to grant to the missionaries and Christians of this country, if you succeed in driving out the Mussulman."

Neither appeal was successful. Emin did not get his invitation (dated 25th August, 1889) until June, 1890; while Jackson had been ordered not to enter Uganda, as the Company feared to compromise the missionaries since Mwanga might think the caravan had been sent to punish him for the death of Hannington.

Jackson's orders were so positive that not even the offer of a trade monopoly in Uganda could tempt him to enter the country, and he continued his geographical explorations to the north-east. Mwanga therefore had to wait until January, 1890, when Stokes came back from the coast with supplies. The war was then at once renewed; the Catholic and Protestant Waganda swore fidelity to each other, if they were victorious, and an immediate attack on Kalema was made. The rival forces met at Bulwanyi on the 11th February; the Mohammedans were routed, and Mwanga re-entered the capital in triumph. Kalema fled to Unyoro, where he subsequently died of smallpox.

Both parties of missionaries at once returned to Uganda. According to Mackay, Père Lourdel stated that the Protestant missionaries were not to be allowed to return, as they had refused to help Mwanga when in exile. This decision, if ever made, was, however, never enforced; but the king was no doubt prejudiced against the Protestants, as he had murdered their bishop, and they had refused to take part in his war. He felt, however, too insecure to dispense with the help of either of the Christian parties, and permitted the English mission to re-occupy its former station.

In February, 1890, there were therefore four parties in Uganda—Catholic, Protestant, Mohammedan, and Pagan. The Catholics were supreme at Court, owing

THE MISSIONARIES RETURN TO UGANDA 171

to the leading share they had taken in Mwanga's restoration, and because the king was nominally a member of their Church. The Protestants distrusted the king, and were jealous of the Catholic supremacy. The Mohammedans, under Kalema, were still powerful, owing to their military organization; but numerically they were weak, and they were under the cloud of recent defeat. Finally, there was the old Pagan party, with which in his heart Mwanga most warmly sympathised. To add to the complication, an expedition under Carl Peters suddenly arrived at the capital, and negotiated a political treaty with Mwanga in the interests of Germany.

Peters, during his raid across Northern British East Africa, reached Kavirondo, and during Jackson's absence visited the British East Africa Company's camp there. The Somali in charge showed Peters the letter in which Père Lourdel appealed to Jackson to enter Uganda and help Mwanga. Peters saw his chance.

He at once wrote to Mwanga and the missionaries, offering his aid, and marched to Uganda. He crossed the Nile on February 20th, 1890. He was met by a letter from Mwanga, written by the Rev. E. C. Gordon, in which he was invited to Mengo, where he was welcomed by the king and the missionaries.

Peters' idea was to make Uganda and the Upper Nile into a neutralized state, like that of the Congo. It was to be open to all Europeans alike. This policy was of course acceptable to the French Fathers, and they supported it warmly. A treaty was signed on 1st March, 1890, between Peters, on behalf of the German Emperor, and Mwanga, by which the latter accepted "the decrees of the Berlin Treaty (Congo Act) of February, 1885, so far as they have reference to Buganda and its tributary countries. He throws open these countries to the subjects of His Majesty the German Emperor, as to all other Europeans. He guarantees to the subjects of His Majesty the German Emperor, as to all other Europeans who may wish to avail themselves of it, entire freedom of trade, and the right of travel and settlement in Buganda and all tributary states."

The English missionaries protested against the treaty, on the ground that Mwanga had already accepted the British protectorate. But the king replied that he had only offered to do so if Jackson helped to restore him to the throne. As he had not been helped by the British, he would not give them the monopoly he had conditionally offered. He now preferred to remain independent, and welcome alike Germans, French, and English.

The time when the neutralization of Uganda had been possible was, however, now past. Mwanga was not unreasonable in considering that his offer had been rejected, and had therefore lapsed. But an agreement

THE MISSIONARIES RETURN TO UGANDA 173

had been already signed in Europe between England and Germany, which placed Uganda in the British sphere. On Peters' return to the coast, he found that his treaty was invalid.

The British East Africa Company was therefore at liberty to occupy and administer Uganda. Jackson accordingly crossed the Nile, and reached Mengo on 14th April, 1890. He signed a treaty with Mwanga, by which the king bowed to the Anglo-German agreement, and Uganda was definitely included in British territory. Jackson shortly afterwards returned to the coast, leaving his comrade, Ernest Gedge, as the Company's representative.

Gedge had a very uncomfortable position. The king would have preferred the neutralization arrangement made with Peters, and Gedge was personally unpopular with both the missionary parties.

The country was simmering with discontent and faction jealousy, and a renewal of civil war seemed imminent. A strong man was wanted in Uganda; and, luckily for the British interests, the right man to deal with the situation was rapidly approaching.

On December 18th, 1890, a badly equipped caravan of some two hundred and seventy men marched into Rubaga under the command of Captain F. D. Lugard

Chapter XI

HOW LUGARD SAVED UGANDA

"Mother earth! are the heroes dead?
  Do they thrill the souls of the years no more?
Are the gleaming snows and the poppies red
  All that is left of the brave of yore?

"Are there none to fight as Theseus fought—
  Far in the young world's misty dream?
Or to teach as the grey-haired Nestor taught?
  Mother earth! are the heroes gone?"

IN 1885 Captain (now General Sir) F. D. Lugard, D.S.O., was entitled to long leave from his regiment, and he resolved to devote it to work in Africa as a volunteer military missionary. It was his ambition, to use his own words, "to embark in some useful undertaking in Africa—if possible, in connection with the suppression of the slave trade." So, with £50 in his pocket, he sailed from Gibraltar to Naples, where he offered his services to the Italians in their Abyssinian enterprise. Finding no opening there, he proceeded to Egypt, but the Egyptian Soudanese policy was closed, and again Lugard's services were rejected. His money was running low, and he felt

HOW LUGARD SAVED UGANDA 175

doubtful whether it would suffice to take him to any field where he could be of use. So he travelled down the Red Sea as a deck passenger on an Italian timber ship. He herded with Arab coolies and Neapolitan roughs, slept on deck among the timber, and had his meals of broken victuals with the Italian cook in the galley beside the engines. He landed at Massowah, and again offered his services to the Italians; but he was again refused. He crossed to Aden, took ship to Quilimane, and went up the Zambesi to help the African Lakes Company in its fight with the Nyasa slavers. His services were here enthusiastically accepted, and he spent twelve months in the campaign. Peace, however, was proclaimed before the slavers had been completely suppressed, and Lugard returned to England to recover from a severe wound. In November, 1889, he was back again on the East Coast, and Mr. G. S. Mackenzie, the administrator of the recently-established British East Africa Company, offered him a post on his staff.

Lugard urged the Company to establish a number of small trading stations, which should be gradually extended inland, from a base on the sea. Thus an effectively occupied and administered wedge would be thrust into the interior. The policy was approved, and Lugard was commissioned to carry it into effect. He founded a chain of posts from Mombasa to the fort at Machakos, which subsequently, under the care of its superintendent, Mr. J. Ainsworth, became the most successful and best administered station in British East Africa.

In May, 1890, Lugard was back at Mombasa, where he set to work on a scheme for the organization of the freed slaves on the coast. There had been a deplorable feud between the Arabs and the missionaries on the slavery question. The missionaries insisted on using their stations as asylums for fugitive slaves, and this proceeding, which was illegal while the coast was under Arab law, naturally roused the enmity of the leading Arab landowners. Lugard, in spite of his very advanced views on the slavery question, realized that the commercial prosperity of the coast planters is essential to the prosperity of British East Africa, and that some allowance should be made for the Arab point of view. He treated the slave-owners with such tact that he secured the enthusiastic co-operation of the Lewali of Melindi and some other leading Arabs in a plan for the solution of the freed-slave difficulty. His work was interrupted by sudden orders to go inland and found a station at the important caravan centre of Ngongo Bagas. He started with a caravan of 150 men and a party of comrades, who, inspired by Lugard's enthusiasm, all made their mark in East African history. The second in command was George Wilson, who ruled Uganda in the troubled time of the mutiny. F. de Winton, who died in Toru, and Grant,

Photo by] GEN. F. D. LUGARD. [*Elliott & Fry*.

now the senior resident and one of the most experienced officers in Uganda, were both on Lugard's staff. The famous Somali, Dualla Idris, was the headman of the caravan, and Shukri Aga, one of Gordon's Soudanese officers, who had returned to the coast with Stanley and Emin, was in charge of the escort. Lugard's force was soon reduced by the desertion of a third of the men, but it was raised to 450 by fresh instalments. It reached Machakos, and Lugard advanced some fifty miles further to the north-west, where he built a new station among the Kikuyu at Dagoreti. But his work was interrupted by the arrival of orders to proceed in hot haste to Uganda, as Stokes "was conveying very large consignments of arms and powder" to that country, and it was necessary to put a stop to this illegal and iniquitous trade.

Wilson was left at Dagoreti; but the Kikuyu were troublesome, and his supplies of ammunition were kept back from him by an officer nearer the coast. Wilson had to abandon the station, which was at once looted and burnt by the natives; he cut his way back to Machakos, where he obtained supplies of ammunition, returned to Dagoreti, and rebuilt the station.

Meanwhile, Lugard was hastening by forced marches to Uganda. As the country was now part of the British Protectorate, he maintained his right to enter without permission. So he marched straight to the capital without waiting for the king's gracious leave.

He reached Mengo on December 18th, 1890, and found to his great relief that he had won the race with Stokes. Lugard's instructions from Sir Francis de Winton, who was the Administrator of British East Africa, warned him that "Mwanga's hope is Stokes, who has promised to bring him large quantities of ammunition, powder, and breech-loading cartridges. With these Mwanga, it is believed, is going to arm the Roman Catholics, and drive the Protestants out." But Stokes had not yet arrived, and the king's position was still somewhat insecure, as he was dependent on his Christian supporters; hence Lugard was in a position to make the king agree to a formal treaty, which was signed on December 26th.

Lugard, however, soon found that he had entered a hornets' nest, owing to the hostility of the four factions — Mohammedan, Protestant, Catholic, and Pagan. The Catholics, having aided Mwanga's restoration, were naturally in favour at Court, and regretted Lugard's arrival.

The Protestants welcomed him, as they expected him to throw in his lot with them against the Catholics. Lugard, however, had no intention of taking sides with one religious party against the rest. As the representative of the British East Africa Company, he considered himself responsible for the administration of the whole country, and felt it was his duty to see that all parties had fair play. His predecessor, Gedge, who had been left behind by Jackson, had tried the same policy, and secured the ill will of both parties of European missionaries. Lugard was soon to suffer the same fate. His arrival threatened the Catholic supremacy, and if he could establish the British East Africa Company in Uganda the French Fathers' plan of an International Free State would be shattered. The Protestant missionaries, on the other hand, were disappointed that Lugard did not at once take their view of the position.

The tension was eased for a while by the arrival of Bishop Tucker, who reached Uganda at the end of December with some new recruits. He had left the coast with seven missionaries, but the treacherous East African climate had killed three of them, had completely shattered the health of a fourth, and reduced the remaining three to so weak a state that on entering Uganda they were unable to walk from the lake shore to the mission station. The Bishop, with his usual fairness and common sense, at once entered into an agreement with Lugard as to the policy of the Church Mission. But the Bishop's stay was short; he could only remain for a month, and so soon as he had left the country his subordinates repudiated the agreement.

At the end of January the British East Africa Company's forces in Uganda were strengthened by the arrival of Captain Williams with seventy-five Soudanese,

100 Zanzibari, and a Maxim gun. Stokes arrived a week later. Lugard immediately protested that Stokes' powder trade was illegal and immoral, and insisted that it must cease. Stokes replied by explaining that he made a profit of £250 on every load (60 lb.) of arms and ammunition that he sold. Lugard did not take the hint, and Stokes, finding that he had mistaken his man, promised to place all his powder in Lugard's keeping; but this promise he forgot to fulfil and soon got the ammunition safely out of Lugard's reach.

Lugard's next care was to reconcile the two Christian factions. The hostility between them was bitter, but it was kept in control by fear of a common enemy, for the Mohammedans and Pagans were still powerful, and might at any time renew the war against the Christians, and perhaps overthrow the king and his allies.

As a first step in the policy of uniting the Christian parties, Lugard persuaded them both to join in an expedition against the Mohammedan faction in Uganda. The alliance was not harmonious, and the preparations for the campaign were marred by continual quarrels. It had been agreed between the two parties that the commander of the Uganda army should be alternately Protestant and Catholic. The Protestants claimed that it was their turn for the command. But the king denied that what the Protestants put in as the previous war with a Catholic in command was a war at all; so he decided that it was the Catholics' turn to nominate the commander-in-chief. These little matters having been arranged, on April 8th the combined forces marched against the Mohammedans. Lugard crossed the Kanyongoro River by a clever stratagem. He pretended to camp, but crossed the river at night and attacked and routed the Mohammedans at dawn on May 7th. He was anxious to follow up the victory by a pursuit of the fugitives and an advance on the capital of Kaberega, the king of Unyoro. The Waganda, however, had had enough of the war, and would not join in the pursuit, so that the fruits of the victory were lost.

The two Christian parties, being thus relieved of the ·common enemy, quarrelled with greater fury than before. Many of the disputes were over trivialities. The main quarrel, however, was respecting the right of the native chiefs to change their religion. That any pagan or Mohammedan could become a Christian was admitted; but the question at issue was whether any Protestant chief could turn Catholic, or *vice versâ*. With the characteristic irony of Uganda politics, the Catholics were for "complete religious liberty," and the Protestants were against it, as they said (*vide, e.g.*, p. 190) the people did not understand it, and that it was useless to give it to them. Lugard reported that "the Catholics behaved very well; they said they were in favour of complete freedom of creed." The Protestants, on the other hand, said that the question was really political and not religious; that the chiefs wanted to change simply because Catholicism was in fashion at court; and, as there had been a division of the chieftainships between the two sects, if men were allowed to change it would upset the recent agreement and balance of power.

On the view, to use Sir Gerald Portal's phrase, that the race for converts in Uganda was synonymous with a race for political power, there is no doubt much to be said for the Protestant position. But to those who look upon missionaries as spiritual teachers the Protestant contention is revolting. That missionaries, sent to preach the gospel that "the truth shall make you free," should, at the end of the nineteenth century, demand that a man should forfeit his position and estates, because he had changed the sect of Christianity to which he belonged, appears simply incredible. It is therefore advisable to state the Protestant position in the words of one of the most respected and most tolerant members of the Church Missionary Society in Uganda. The Rev. R. H. Walker, in a letter dated 14th July, 1891, to the *Church Missionary Intelligencer*, explains the Protestant case as follows :—

"Now many want to leave the Protestant party, and to join that of the king, because they get more honour by doing so. The Protestants agree to their

HOW LUGARD SAVED UGANDA 183

leaving and becoming Catholics, but say, of course, they leave their offices or territories behind them when they change parties. Some consider it unfair to make a man give up his position in the country because he changes his religion. The Catholics fall in with this, as it will increase the power of their party in the land."

In this controversy Lugard sided with the Protestants on the ground that the whole struggle between the two parties was political and not religious. He declined to speak of them as Catholic and Protestant, but as French and English, although the "French" Bishop was a German, and one of the "French" priests (Père Gaudibert) was an Englishman.

Lugard's decision for a while led to a decrease in avowed defections to the Catholic cause. But he saw quite clearly that the Catholics, or, as he called them, the Wa-Fransi (*i.e.*, the French), were rapidly gaining overwhelming strength. The refusal of Jackson and the English missionaries to help Mwanga during his war of restoration had thrown him into the hands of the Catholics, and the Protestants were steadily losing in numbers and power.

Lugard foresaw that, as soon as the Catholics were sufficiently sure of their position, they would endeavour to expel the Protestants. Even if the Company could afford to send further reinforcements from the coast they could not arrive in time; and, to hold Uganda against the Catholics, Lugard knew to be impossible with the forces at his disposal.

While Lugard was puzzling over the best course to adopt, it occurred to him that somewhere to the west of Uganda there was a body of Emin Pasha's old Egyptian troops, who might be called to the rescue. They were part of the force which had held the Equatorial Soudan against the Mahdists, and had been left behind, when Emin and Stanley withdrew from the Soudan.

It is true that Selim Bey, Emin's most trustworthy officer, had been sent to bring these people to Kavalli's, and Stanley had waited for them as long as he had felt justified. He allowed Selim what he thought ample time, and it might have been ample for Stanley. But Selim Bey was not a Stanley, and he did not keep his appointment. Stanley accused him of intentional delay; and, as some of the other Soudanese officers had been guilty of treachery to Emin, Lugard hesitated about bringing Selim and his men into Uganda. But Shukri, the head of the Soudanese with Lugard, was positive that Selim had done his best, and that the garrisons around Wadelai had been so scattered that it was impossible to collect them in the time allowed. Shukri Aga insisted most strongly that Selim Bey was, and always had been, loyal;

that he had been most eager to accompany the "relief expedition" to the coast, but would not desert his men. He had appealed for a little longer time, but before he reached Kavalli's the "Emin Expedition" had left for the coast and Selim and his people were left stranded on the shores of the Albert Nyanza. Lugard was at length convinced that Selim could be trusted. He knew his own position in Uganda was untenable with the forces at his command, and that it was hopeless to ask for assistance from the coast, so he resolved to visit Selim Bey and invite his help.

At the end of the Mohammedan war Lugard therefore left Captain Williams in charge of Uganda and marched westward to the Albert Nyanza. He went first to Toru, a district at the eastern foot of Ruwenzori, that had once been an independent Wahuma kingdom. It had been recently conquered by its northern neighbours, the Wanyoro, who continually raided the country to pillage and enslave. Kasagama, the son of the last king of Toru, was a fugitive in Uganda, so Lugard took him back and replaced him on his father's throne.

Kasagama was warmly welcomed by his people; Lieutenant de Winton was left to build a series of forts and to protect the country from the Wanyoro, and Lugard continued westward on his errand to Selim.

He found the Soudanese settlement, and he explained

to Selim the difficulties in Uganda and begged him to prevent the expulsion of the British.

Selim told Lugard the story of his adventures since he had been sent to Wadelai to collect the last of the Soudanese garrisons. He explained that he had been unable to rejoin Stanley in the ten weeks allotted him, because one of the garrisons he had to bring back was a month's march from Wadelai. After many difficulties he reached Kavalli's a few days after Stanley had left. Fadl Maula, the Soudanese officer who had organized the mutiny against Emin, then sent a force to attack Kavalli's. The rebel Soudanese took Selim prisoner, looted the station, and returned north to Wadelai. Selim was released and left with 90 men and 300 women and children in a state of utter destitution. He settled at Kavalli's, where he was attacked by the natives, and in the fight lost half his men. But the chief Kavalli interfered and saved his force from annihilation.

Meanwhile Fadl Maula, who was now in command of almost the whole of the Soudanese, played false to his own men. He entered into an intrigue to compel his force to submit to the Mahdists. His men discovered the plot, repelled a Mahdist attack, and then marched south to join Selim. They left Wadelai in March, 1891, and reached Kavalli's forty days later.

By this reinforcement Selim had under his command a force of 600 Soudanese troops, the survivors of over 3,000, and was now safe from attack by the natives. He planted cotton seeds, made rough handlooms, wove cloth for uniforms, and tried to re-establish among his men the discipline and organization of civilized troops.

In July, 1891, he was visited by Emin Pasha, who, now in the service of the German Government, came to Kavalli's, hoping to persuade Selim and the Soudanese to enlist under the German flag. A few consented, but, owing to Selim's influence, the Soudanese, as a body, remained faithful to their Egyptian allegiance and refused to enter the German service. Emin went away disappointed, and his few Soudanese recruits deserted at the first opportunity.

Lugard's proposals, however, Selim regarded with favour. He had been one of Gordon's officers, and expressed himself devoted to the British. He asked for time to think over the invitation, and terms were discussed. Lugard suggested that some other Soudanese should take part in the conference, but Selim replied "that he alone would decide for his people, and what he resolved on they would do." "And so," adds Lugard, "it eventually turned out."

Selim's main hesitation was that he was an Egyptian soldier, and that he did not like to enlist in a foreign service without authorization. He declared that "he had grown grey in the service of the Khedive, and that nothing should induce him to swerve in his allegiance to the flag for which he had a hundred times risked his life."

To wait for permission from Egypt would have rendered Selim's assistance useless. So the enlistment took place on the understanding that the Khedive's consent was to be obtained at the earliest possible opportunity, and that, if the Khedive withheld it, Selim and his men should be immediately released from their engagement. Further, it was decided that, until the Khedive's reply came, the Soudanese should not be sent to the southern Soudan, or beyond the northern and north-western frontiers of Unyoro. Lugard also agreed that all orders to the Soudanese should be given through Selim Bey.

The alliance was popular with the Soudanese, who were delighted at the prospect of return to active service. A review was held, and the troops marched in column before Lugard, carrying their old Egyptian flags.

"It was impossible," says Lugard, "not to feel a thrill of admiration for these deserted soldiers, as they carried past flag after flag, torn and riddled in many fierce engagements with the Mahdists."

The terms of enlistment having been settled, Lugard returned to Rubaga, the capital of Uganda, with a Soudanese force sufficient to quell any rebellion that might arise. The British position in Uganda seemed at length secure.

HOW LUGARD SAVED UGANDA 189

However, on Christmas Day, 1891, a mail came in from the coast with orders that Uganda was to be evacuated, and the Company's forces were to return at once to the coast. "This is a thunderbolt," said Lugard. The order came to him as a crushing surprise. Since his departure he had had but few chances of communication with the coast, and he was not aware that the British East Africa Company had reached a financial crisis. It found itself unable to maintain the expense of holding Uganda; and it had no option but to withdraw. Lugard was in a painful dilemma. Both he and Williams had given their personal assurance to their Waganda allies that England would not abandon them, and they felt that obedience to the Company's order would be an act of personal treachery. On the other hand, to retain the Zanzibari when the Company could not pay their wages would be equally bad faith with them. Lugard was relieved by a noble offer from Captain Williams, who generously undertook to pay personally the expenses of the retention of Uganda, until an appeal could be sent to the coast.

A fortnight later (7th January, 1892) came the news that Sir William Mackinnon and some of the friends of the Church Missionary Society had subscribed sufficient funds to pay for a year's administration of Uganda, in the hope that by that time the Company would be able to pay its way, and permanently retain the country.

But the news that the Company was in sore straits,

and that Lugard had been actually ordered to return, was known to the Catholics, and added greatly to Lugard's difficulties. It destroyed the Company's prestige, and shook the confidence of its allies.

During Lugard's absence, moreover, the bitterness between the two Christian parties had been intensified. Williams, unaware of Lugard's decision, refused to enforce the confiscation of the property of those Protestants who had turned Catholic. Captain Williams was a straightforward, outspoken soldier, with a typical Englishman's distrust of plausible excuses for deviation from what appears the honest policy. He flatly refused to confiscate any man's property as a punishment for change of creed. For this he was bitterly attacked by the Protestants, who threatened a war in consequence. One of the Church missionaries (the late Rev. G. L. Pilkington) declared that war was almost inevitable, and threw the blame on Williams. "The probability of war," he wrote, "was caused by a proposal from Captain Williams to abolish the agreement made between the two parties, and to permit chiefs—all of whom now hold office *qua* Protestant or Roman Catholic, appointed by one or other party—who change their religion to retain their chieftainships. We should, of course, be delighted to see full religious liberty, but the people do not understand it, and the Protestant party were very resolute against accepting the proposal."

The English missionaries sent Williams a strongly-worded protest, and wrote to England complaining that he was ruling "Uganda through the priests." They said that he had shown gross partiality to the Catholics, and had purposely weakened the Protestants in order to favour the Catholics. The best answer to this charge is the fact that the Catholics were equally wrathful with Williams for favouring the Protestants. The French bishop protested, in a letter written on 23rd January, that during Williams' administration the Catholics could "no longer obtain any justice, and the thing has come to such a pass that they do not even think of going any more to the fort at Kampala with their grievances."

Thus, while the Catholics declared they were staying away from the fort owing to Williams' gross partiality to the Protestants, one, at least, of the English missionaries would not enter the fort owing to Williams' gross partiality to the Catholics.

Lugard therefore returned to Uganda to find religious bitterness worse than when he had left for the Albert Nyanza. Feelings on both sides were so excited that it was evident that the slightest untoward accident would precipitate a civil war. Lugard did his best to prevent an outbreak, as is admitted by one of his severest critics. "It is impossible," says Ashe, "to speak too highly of Lugard's earnest desire for peace, or of his patience and forbearance under the most trying circumstances; and I feel sure that, had peace been possible, no man that has ever entered Uganda was more fitted to secure it."

But all efforts for peace were in vain. Both sides were arming, and Protestant and Catholic natives began gun-stealing from each other in their feverish preparations. A Catholic, whose gun had been stolen by a Protestant, appealed for its return from the chief whose follower had stolen it. He could get no redress, and resolved to take compensation by stealing a gun from the other side. He entered into a long palaver with a Protestant about the sale of some beer, and while the bargaining was going on, an accomplice snatched the Protestant's gun and fled with it into the adjacent compound of a Catholic named Mugoloba. The Protestant gave chase, and tried to force his way into the enclosure, whereupon he was shot dead by the owner.

The different accounts vary in details, but they agree in the essential facts. The Protestants demanded vengeance on Mugoloba; but the king ruled that, according to Uganda law, a man was justified in shooting any one who was trying forcibly to enter his enclosure.

The law on the subject is, perhaps, doubtful. Had the Protestant entered the enclosure at night, Mugoloba would have been unquestionably within his rights in shooting the trespasser. As the incident occurred during daylight, the Protestant party declared their man had a perfect right to force his way after the thief. The Church Missionary Society's report describes the affair as "the cold-blooded murder of a Protestant chief." There was not much cold blood circulating in the veins of the Waganda at this time.

Lugard, however, thought the king's decision unfair, and protested against it. His protest was ignored, and he was himself treated with insult and ridicule by the Catholic chiefs present during his interview with the king.

Lugard saw that war was imminent. He appealed to the Catholic bishop for help in averting it; but the reply showed Lugard that the Catholics would do nothing to prevent an outbreak of hostilities. They knew their party was strongest amongst the natives, and probably thought they had everything to gain by a fight. To be ready for emergencies, Lugard at once served out to the Protestants forty guns and some powder. Next day the war drums were beaten, and both sides were drawn up in line of battle, waving flags of defiance.

The capital of Uganda is built upon four hills. The southern hill is known as Mengo, the seat of the king's palace, and the ancient capital of Uganda. A little to the north-west of Mengo is the hill of Rubaga, which is the headquarters of the Catholic Mission.

The Protestant Mission has its station on the hill of Namirembe, which is due north of Mengo. The eastern hill, Kampala, is crowned by the British fort, and was the headquarters of the Company.

The Catholics had concentrated on Mengo, in front of the king's palace, while the Protestant forces were mainly collected on the hill around the English Mission buildings of Namirembe, and opposite the French Mission station at Rubaga. The fighting is said by Lugard to have begun by the Catholics suddenly opening fire. The Protestants at once attacked Rubaga, where there was only the weak left wing of the Catholic army to oppose them. The Protestants easily captured the hill, and set fire to the Catholic church and station. The Catholics, in turn, advanced north from Mengo towards Kampala. Lugard concluded that they were going to attack the fort, and accordingly opened fire with the Maxim at a distance of 1,400 yards. The fire was effective. The Catholics fled, after about a dozen had been wounded and half a dozen killed.

After a little more fighting, Williams charged with the Soudanese, and the Catholic army was driven from the field. The Protestants commenced to loot and burn, in spite of the strenuous efforts of the English officers.

The king fled to Bulingugwe, a small island seven miles from the capital. Lugard was anxious to get him back to Mengo, where he could be kept under control and out of mischief. He asked Mwanga to return, and allowed the Catholic bishop to go to Bulingugwe on the promise that he would do his best to bring the king back. But the bishop's promise, according to Ashe, was "a diplomatic ruse to obtain his own liberty"; for, as soon as the bishop reached the king, he urged him not to return to Mengo. Lugard then sent Stokes' headman, Mafitaa, on the same errand. He reported that the king was anxious to get home again, but was kept a prisoner by the Catholics. Accordingly, on the 28th January, Lugard sent an ultimatum demanding Mwanga's return. He could not allow so large a force to remain in his rear, while he might at any time be attacked by the Mohammedan party from the north.

On the very next day (January 29th) some of the king's party attacked some Protestant canoes, which were taking food from the island of Komi to the mainland. This renewed act of war, combined with an insulting message from the king, showed Lugard that strong steps must be taken. On the following day he sent Williams with a Maxim gun and a hundred Soudanese, under Dualla, to attack Bulingugwe. The island was less than a quarter of a mile from the mainland, so that it was within range of the Maxim. At two in the afternoon Dualla, with fifteen canoes, crossed the strait under shelter of the Maxim fire. The Catholics were panic-stricken. The king and the bishop escaped in a canoe, and the people tried to follow them. The canoes were overcrowded, many of them sank, and in the flight some hundreds of the natives were drowned.

Mwanga and the Catholic bishop, who, it may be remembered, was a German, fled across the lake to German territory. The king took up his residence at the Catholic station of Bukumbi, where, according to Ashe, he was "watched, as a mouse is watched by a cat, by his Roman Catholic subjects, who were now really his gaolers." Mwanga soon tired of Catholicism when it meant exile, and on March 30th he escaped from the station and returned to Mengo, where he was respectfully welcomed by Lugard and reinstated as king. But he now fully realized that his absolute power was at an end, and that in future he must reign as a vassal of the British East Africa Company. He accepted a treaty with Lugard, which made this position perfectly clear. In this treaty Lugard stipulated that the missionaries should confine themselves to missionary work, and one clause defined their proper sphere of work as "preaching the Gospel, and teaching the arts and industries of civilization." But this ruling was not in accordance with the views of the missionaries, although non-interference in politics is one of the accepted rules of the Church Missionary Society. The President of the Protestant Mission at once repudiated the idea that he should not interfere in politics; he maintained "that the Protestant chiefs were now the rulers of Uganda, and that Lugard's treaty only enabled him to rule through the king and chiefs."

The Catholics were almost as hostile as their rivals, for they were angry at their complete overthrow. And while Ashe accused Lugard of being "entirely under the influence of the fascinating fathers," he was equally accused by them of gross injustice. Indeed, both missionary parties for a while lost their own jealousies in hatred of Lugard, whom they denounced as a murderer and a liar.

"Penal servitude, free from missionaries, were a state of comparative bliss," exclaimed Lugard in despair.

This feud at the capital between the Company and the missionaries inspired the Mohammedans with the hope that they might recover their supremacy, and they prepared to attack Mengo.

Lugard resolved to try diplomacy, and sent Selim Bey to treat with Mbogo, the Mohammedan Sultan. Selim did his work so well that Mbogo was persuaded to give up his claims to the Uganda throne, and to meet Lugard at a conference. Mbogo was at first afraid to enter Uganda, as he suspected treachery; but Selim swore on the Koran that he would be responsible for his safety. Mbogo met Lugard at a conference, and was induced to settle at Kampala. A treaty was arranged, which assigned to the Mohammedans the three provinces—Kitunzi, Katambala, and Kasuju.

Meanwhile the Christians, annoyed at this peaceful settlement with the Mohammedans, were again meditating mischief; for the Protestants projected an alliance with the Catholics for a treacherous attack on the Company's forces. But the Soudanese garrison rendered Lugard's position impregnable, and the last scheme for Lugard's overthrow came to nought.

Lugard had now firmly established the Company's position in Uganda. He had routed the Catholics, made peace with the Mohammedans, and enlisted a garrison of Soudanese, who rendered him independent of the Protestants. He had demonstrated that Uganda could be held, and had maintained British supremacy throughout a greater crisis than was likely to recur. The future of Uganda was now financial, and the question of its retention must be fought out in England. So in June, 1892, Lugard started for the coast, leaving Williams in charge of Uganda.

In Captain Williams' hands the British supremacy was absolutely secure. His relations to the Protestant missionaries were, however, even more bitter than had been those of Lugard. Though politically opposed to the Catholics, his personal relations with them were more cordial. In February, 1893, he attacked the Wavuma islanders to punish some acts of piracy. Otherwise his administration was peaceful, and he kept the country in order till the end of the period for which the British East Africa Company had agreed to continue the occupation of Uganda.

Chapter XII

UGANDA UNDER THE FOREIGN OFFICE

"Fate had set me down in the very furthest point from all civilization, as a captain of Bashi-bazouks, a raider and an ivory thief."
—*The Commandant of Unyoro*, 1895.

THE establishment of the direct Foreign Office control over Uganda, which was informally effected by Sir Gerald Portal on 1st April, 1893, was the result of a vigorous agitation in England during the autumn and early winter of 1892. The movement for the Imperial occupation of Uganda was begun by the English missionary party, and by the friends of the East Africa Company. They received the powerful support of Sir H. M. Stanley. But the success of the movement was in the main due to the powerful appeals of Captain Lugard. He left Uganda in June, 1892, and landed in England in October. He opened the campaign by a paper to the Geographical Society, and followed this pronouncement by an energetic agitation on the platform and in the press. He urged the commercial value of Uganda, the commanding strategic position of the country, and the damage that would be done to British prestige if we abandoned our allies and converts to the persecutions of their foes. The advocates for the retention of Uganda no doubt had the sympathy of the permanent officials of the Foreign Office, and the support of the Foreign Secretary, Lord Rosebery. But the policy was strongly opposed by those who considered British East Africa economically worthless, and that entanglement in adventures there would tie our hands in the struggle for more profitable fields. This party was weak numerically, but it was strong in political influence; for it was maintaining the traditional Liberal principles which were still held by some of the strongest members of the existing Government, including Sir William Harcourt, then the Leader of the House of Commons.

As the popular agitation for the retention of Uganda increased in strength, the section of the ministry in favour of this policy became more resolute. Neither side would give way, and it was evident that something must be done to prevent a split in the Cabinet. So to postpone discussion of the question until after the end of the parliamentary session of 1893, it was resolved to send Sir Gerald Portal, the British Consul-General at Zanzibar, to Uganda—to write a report.

The decision was formed in December, 1892. It was a ten weeks' march to Uganda; for the sake of appearances, the commissioner ought to devote at least

THE UGANDA RAILWAY : MAKUPA BRIDGE.
(*Connecting Mombasa Island with the Mainland.*)

two months to his investigations in the country; ten weeks would be occupied in the return journey to Zanzibar, and another three on the journey home. Hence, by this simple appointment of a commissioner, whose report could not be received in England until the end of August, the Government removed Uganda from the field of parliamentary discussion in the session of 1893.

Sir Gerald Portal thoroughly understood what was expected of him. He remarked before he started that he could as well write his report at once in Zanzibar as he could in Uganda, for the essential facts were all known. But an immediate report was precisely what was not wanted. So on the 3rd January, 1893, he and his staff left Mombasa, and began the weary march on the long Uganda Road. The monotony of the journey, however, was varied by shooting some rhinoceros and some Kikuyu.

The instructions sent to Portal by Lord Rosebery were extremely vague. Portal was "to frame a report as expeditiously as may be, on the best means of dealing with the country, whether through Zanzibar or otherwise." Portal clearly shows that he understood that his nominal duty was to report regarding "the retention or evacuation of Uganda."

He entered Kampala on 17th March, and immediately opened negotiations with both the missionary parties and the king.

Sir Gerald Portal found the two mission parties still bitterly opposed. He reported (8th April) though there had been no further outbreak of hostilities since the previous spring, "nevertheless that peace could not yet be looked upon as being permanent or assured. The Catholics were arming rapidly, and sparing no sacrifice in their effort to obtain a supply of arms and ammunition, and that they were in a dangerous state of discontent."

Portal's report to the Government threw the blame for the Uganda disasters on the unfortunate mixture of religious and political parties. "The miserable history of Uganda for the last two years is sufficient to show how inextricably religion and politics are interwoven in this country, and I fear that the narrow, fanatical nature of the people forbids us to hope for any great improvement in this respect for several years to come."

He found Uganda divided into three factions, nominally religious, but in reality political—the Mohammedan, under Mbogo, and the two Christian parties, of which the real leaders were the European missionaries. "That the missionaries, on both sides, are the veritable political leaders of their respective factions, there can be no doubt whatever." Portal considered this fact as deplorable as it was indisputable. He admitted that it would have been difficult for the missionaries to have avoided acquiring the political leadership. But neither

UGANDA UNDER THE FOREIGN OFFICE

party wanted to avoid acquiring political power, so it was not to be expected that they should have exercised "the very great tact and judgment" by which, according to Portal, they could have kept aloof from political strife. Portal bluntly reported "that the race for converts now being carried on by the Catholic and Protestant missions in Uganda is synonymous with a race for political power." He asserted that it was only the presence of the English officers and the Soudanese troops at the fort that kept peace between the two Christian factions; and he predicted that, if the British administration were withdrawn, "the war of extermination will be at once renewed." He deplored that "no doctrine of toleration, if it has been taught on either side, appears to have been received by the native Christians." And this religious intolerance, according to Portal, has, "since the introduction of the two forms of Christianity into Uganda, cost many hundreds of lives, and has thrown the country fifty years back in its advance towards prosperity. It is deeply to be regretted that the avowedly great influence of missionaries in Uganda is not used to introduce a spirit of tolerance and peace, even at the risk of loss to the party of some political power, or a few wealthy chieftainships."

Portal accordingly concluded that British occupation was necessary to prevent the outbreak of a civil war of extermination, and that it was the main duty of the

British administrator to reconcile the two parties, or at least keep the peace between them, by holding the balance of power. With difficulty he persuaded the two bishops to agree to a division of Uganda into Protestant and Catholic provinces; this arrangement was only rendered possible by the courageous concessions and moderation of Bishop Tucker. By the treaty the Catholics were restored to several important political appointments, and were given the province of Kamia, the Island of Sesse, the district of Luwekula, and the plantations of Mwanika through Majama to the capital, in addition to the province of Budu, which had belonged to them in accordance with Lugard's treaty.

To strengthen the administration, Portal enlisted 450 Soudanese, and established them at Ntebbi, a station on the shore of the Nyanza a few miles from the capital.

Portal's third measure was to reverse Lugard's western policy by abandoning the chain of forts built to protect Toru from the raids of the Wanyoro. The withdrawal of these garrisons was an unfortunate mistake; and though this step was promptly reversed after Portal's departure, it was attended with disastrous consequences.

Portal stayed for two months in Uganda, and when he left for home the outlook was more peaceful than it had been for some time before. The two Christian parties were cowed into submission; the Mohammedan

UGANDA UNDER THE FOREIGN OFFICE

question appeared to have been completely settled by Lugard's arrangement; the capital of Uganda was garrisoned by a Soudanese force under an officer with a long record of faithful service. Yet in less than three weeks from Portal's departure, on the 30th May, Uganda was again enjoying a political crisis, and the whole of the Soudanese garrison was being disarmed on a charge of mutiny.

When Portal started on his return journey, he left Captain (now Colonel Sir) J. R. L. Macdonald temporarily in charge. Macdonald was an Indian railway officer, who had been sent to East Africa in 1892 to survey the projected railway from Mombasa to the Victoria Nyanza. He was returning from this work, when he was ordered back to Uganda to report on the charges made by the French missionaries against Lugard's administration. His report has never been published, but it is believed to have been hostile to Lugard, as the English Government agreed to pay the exorbitant demands of the Catholics for their losses in the war. As Macdonald was the senior officer in Uganda on Portal's departure, he was left as acting commissioner, with instructions to interfere as little as possible in internal politics.

Portal's readjustment of the provinces of the Catholics and Protestants had rendered the Mohammedans discontented with their share. They sent in a claim for more lands, which was received in Kampala after

Portal's departure. The Mohammedans threatened to refuse to pay their taxes, until their asserted wrongs were righted. Their demands were refused, and trouble looked inevitable. On 16th June Selim Bey sent a message to the administrator, intended to prevent an outbreak of hostilities. The message was verbal, and there are grave doubts as to the accuracy of its translation. Macdonald's own version is as follows: "The message was to the effect that he [Selim] heard that there was a probability of a fight between the king Mwanga and the Uganda Mohammedans; that he had told Mbogo [the Mohammedan chief] not to fight, but warned me that if I allowed the king Mwanga to fight the Mohammedans, that he, Selim Bey, as he and Captain Lugard had brought the Waganda Mohammedans into the country, would consider hostile action on the part of Mwanga against the Waganda Mohammedans as hostile action against himself."

For a native officer to tell his political superior that he would treat any act as hostile was of course an irregular proceeding. But we must remember that the Mohammedans had strongly objected to re-entering Uganda, and that they had only consented to return after Selim Bey had sworn on the Koran that no harm should happen to them. He had pledged his personal honour to the Mohammedans, and it was not surprising, therefore, that he should have endeavoured to secure the peaceable redress of their grievances.

Selim's message, whether understood correctly or not, created great excitement in Kampala. Macdonald interpreted it as a threat of rebellion, and feared that the Soudanese troops would mutiny. He arrested Mbogo and other Mohammedan leaders, called as many as possible of the Europeans into the fort, and disarmed the Soudanese troops. Selim was then arrested at Port Alice. There was no trouble over the arrests. Mbogo's Mohammedan supporters were sent away peacefully by their leader; Selim offered no resistance; and the troops at Ntebbi laid down their arms, saying, according to Ashe, " We obey, because Selim, our leader, has asked us to do so." A slight skirmish between some of the Waganda Mohammedans and some Protestants was the only fight in connection with this deplorable episode.

Selim was placed on his trial for treason and mutinous conduct. The evidence against him was his message to Macdonald. It is now generally admitted that the message was mistranslated, as Mr. Reddie, to whom it was given, had then a limited knowledge of Suahili. Selim emphatically repudiated the statements attributed to him. Nevertheless, though the charge of treason was abandoned, Selim was convicted of insubordination. He was degraded, and marched away in irons to the coast. Selim was slowly dying of dropsy, and this treatment no doubt hastened his death. He died before reaching Naivasha, his end embittered by what he regarded as an ungrateful return for his years of faithful service.

Whether Selim deserved his fate depends on the question whether he was guilty of mutiny. The statement that there was any mutiny at all is dismissed by Sir Gerald Portal in his official report on the occurrence, for he says that " Captain Macdonald appears to have taken every precaution in anticipation of the complications which *might have ensued in the event of a mutiny of the Soudanese.*"

The evidence of the missionaries, who have been uniformly hostile to the Soudanese, is less explicit; but their chief spokesman, Mr. Ashe, remarks that there was "nothing secretly treacherous in his [Selim's] action," and whether he meant to resort to arms against the Government " it is a little difficult to decide."

That Selim should have mutinied is in itself highly improbable. Most of the Europeans who had come in contact with him describe him as an honest, well-meaning, but indolent man.

Stanley was certainly not prejudiced in his favour, for he was irritated with his slowness and what he called his dense stupidity. Stanley's graphic sketch of Selim is a tribute to his honesty.

" He is six feet high, large of girth, about fifty years old, black as coal; I am rather inclined to like him. The malignant and deadly conspirator is always lean. I read in this man's face indolence, a tendency to pet

UGANDA UNDER THE FOREIGN OFFICE

his animalism. He is a man to be led, not to conspire. Feed him with good things to eat and plenty to drink, Selim Bey would be faithful. Ah, the sleepy eye of the full-stomached man. This is a man to eat and sleep and snore and play the sluggard in bed, to dawdle slip-shod in the bed-chamber, to call for coffee fifty times a day and native beer by the gallon, to sip and sip and smile, and then to sleep again, and so and so to his grave."

Stanley's officer, Jephson, who had even better opportunities of knowing Selim intimately, tells us that "he was enormously fat and broad. He was a great, easy-going fellow, with a good-natured, cherubic face, and had a little shrew of a wife who kept him in splendid order."

These descriptions, written years before the trouble in Uganda, do not represent Selim as the type of man who would start a mutiny on his death-bed. And the testimonies to Selim's fidelity of character are equally strong. Jephson reports that, when the rebellion against Emin broke out among the Soudanese, Selim did his best to restrain the soldiers and save Emin, and he warned the rebel officers to do nothing violent. Selim was chosen by Emin to act as his intermediary with the rebels; he smuggled letters to Emin and Jephson when they were prisoners, telling them of Stanley's arrival on the Albert Nyanza; and he finally secured their release.

Selim also held a good record for valiant service in the field. By his bravery at Dufilé he rallied the troops and broke the Dervish attack, and thus saved Emin, the last of Gordon's governors, from being carried captive to Khartoum.

Lugard's testimony to Selim's loyalty in Uganda is emphatic. Lugard found him absolutely loyal and devoted in his allegiance to the Khedive and to the English. After Lugard got to know him, he trusted him implicitly, and was rewarded by assistance which Lugard describes as invaluable. We can therefore understand Lugard's burning indignation that the man who did most to hold the Equatorial Provinces against the Mahdists, and in truth saved the English from being driven from Uganda—that such a man should have been done to death in chains and disgrace, for a share in what Portal apparently regarded as a phantom mutiny.

"Recent telegrams," says Lugard, "bring the news that Selim Bey has been convicted by Captain Macdonald of treachery, and of an intrigue with the Mohammedan Waganda, having for its object the overthrow of the British. Judging by the accounts which have reached England, Selim's open defiance, when he thought the Mohammedans unjustly treated, can hardly be called 'treachery.' He was at the time dying of dropsy, but was ordered to march to the coast, and, of course, died. The story I have told will show that, at the risk of his own life, Selim remained loyal to me; that it was mainly owing to him that the settlement with the Mohammedans was effected—at a time when, had he desired to act treacherously, the opportunity was before him. The Soudanese in Toru were close by, and would have followed him blindly; the whole Mohammedan Waganda faction would have eagerly accepted the chance. He remained absolutely loyal; and I knew the man with whom I was dealing well enough to know that it would be so. There must have been a strange want of tact to convert a loyalty so sincere into hostility, when Selim was even then a dying man. . . . To me it is a sad contemplation that this veteran selected by Gordon for the command of Mruli, whose valour saved Dufilé, against whom no charge of disloyalty had ever yet been proved amidst all the faithlessness of the Soudan troops, and who had proved at the risk of his life his loyalty to me—that this man should have been hurried off in a dying state, discredited and disgraced, to succumb on the march, a prisoner and an outcast."

The death of Selim Bey is one of the most pathetic episodes in the history of the Foreign Office rule in Uganda, and its subsequent effects were deplorable. The Soudanese, however, remained loyal, and they were soon re-armed and used in furtherance of the active policy that was adopted in Uganda.

The principles of the policy on which Sir Gerald

Portal had decided were reserve and experiment. It was a mark-time policy to discover the minimum cost at which Uganda could be held. Sufficient Soudanese were to be enlisted to defend Kampala and enable the Commissioner to hold the balance of power between the three Waganda parties. The outlying forts, which Lugard had built to protect Toru from the Wanyoro, were abandoned; the British Acting Commissioner was ordered not to interfere in the internal administration of Uganda, except to prevent gross injustice or cruelty or the renewal of internal war, and he was to undertake no act of aggression against the neighbouring states.

But Sir Gerald Portal's system was almost immediately abandoned by his successors. In November, 1893, Macdonald was superseded by the arrival of Colonel (now General Sir Henry) Colvile. Colvile found that a campaign had already been prepared against the people of Unyoro, who had raided into Toru as soon as Lugard's chain of forts had been removed by Sir Gerald Portal. The reason for the recall of the garrison was because they were not under European supervision, and were ill-treating the population they were supposed to protect. That the Soudanese were not treating their neighbours as they would themselves have liked to be treated is most probable. The only question is which particular section of the native population was their victim. According to Ashe the

Soudanese were raiding the natives of Southern Unyoro by order of Kasagama, the king of Toru. If Ashe be correct, then the king of Unyoro can hardly be blamed for punishing Kasagama as soon as the Soudanese garrisons were recalled to Uganda.

The justice of the war against Unyoro is therefore open to doubt. But Macdonald had decided on the war and already prepared for it. As Colvile naturally did not care to upset his predecessor's arrangements the campaign was begun. A combined Soudanese and Waganda army marched from Kampala ten days after Colvile's arrival. The affair, according to Thruston, was not worthy of being called a war; he describes it in a chapter of his book headed "Chasse aux Nègres," explaining that he accepted the truth of the epigram of a French traveller, "On ne fait pas la guerre en Afrique; ce qui s'y fait, c'est la chasse aux Nègres."

The army, which consisted of some 15,000 to 20,000 men, started from Unyoro on 4th December, 1893. Colvile took Mwanga with him, partly to give him a pleasant holiday, and partly to keep him out of mischief while the Commissioner was away. Resistance on the part of the Wanyoro was useless. Their capital was taken and burnt, many of the peasantry were shot, but there was no decisive or exciting engagement. Colvile formed a low opinion of the military qualities of his Waganda allies, though, according to Thruston, their tactics were extremely skilful whenever they left the main expedition and began cattle-lifting on their own account.

After a fruitless chase of the king, the expedition returned to Uganda in February, 1894, Colvile leaving Major Thruston, Dr. Moffat and Mr. Forster, with a garrison of 660 men, to administer Unyoro. The three men did their work as well as such work could be done. To raid into a country, to seize all the ivory and cattle that can be found, and then to retreat with the loot, is the traditional African system of warfare. Colvile's raid on Unyoro therefore appeared to the Wanyoro as part of the established order of the universe. But that a few men should be left to hold the country permanently was not part of the ordinary game.

The necessity for the occupation of Unyoro was due to the fact that the only way in which Colvile could pay his Waganda allies was by giving them some of the best estates in Unyoro. He accordingly presented a large tract of country south of Mruli to the Protestants, and assigned the Catholics a smaller, but still extensive, district known as Kikakure, west of the province of Singo.

The Waganda settled in the regions allotted to them; they killed the men, and seized all the women they could find. Those who could escape fled to the Wakedi country, whence they waged a guerilla warfare against their Waganda supplanters. The British garrison was established at the fort of Hoima, which was frequently beleaguered by the natives. The monthly caravans from Uganda had to fight their way through the enemy. Stray parties of Soudanese and British friendlies were cut off and slain, and in retaliation the villages and plantations near the scene of action were destroyed.

When Colvile entered Unyoro it was one of the richest food countries in Eastern Equatorial Africa, it had a considerable population, and it was a very important trade centre. Colvile himself tells us that "from the capital to Kibba the country had been one mass of banana groves, sweet potato and bean fields." The prolonged guerilla warfare, that began in 1894, devastated the most fertile districts of Unyoro; crops were cut down before the grain had formed, plantations went out of cultivation, the native trade routes were closed. Famine was therefore inevitable, and after a spell of famine pestilence swept through the country. It has been estimated that in the four years following the establishment of British rule the population was reduced to a fourth.

But all this time, it must be remembered, England had not annexed Unyoro, so that the military occupation was somewhat irregular.

Lord Kimberley, as Secretary for Foreign Affairs, once assured the House of Lords that Unyoro had not been annexed, and that the natives were not under British protection. This declaration was read at the mess table at Hoima, the headquarters in Unyoro, and called forth the remark that it was not easy to understand the first part of the statement, but that the natives were not under British protection was quite correct, for "we shoot them all at sight."

There can be little doubt that the policy being carried out in Central Africa was not approved by the Home Government. It wanted the country ruled cheaply, and these wars were very costly, and the Liberal party had always been hostile to wars of aggression and unnecessary extensions of our frontiers. But no efficient check was possible, owing to the slowness of communications with Uganda. The Government mildly rebuked Colvile's forward policy; but the message did not arrive until Colvile had left for England in December 1894.

The new Commissioner in Uganda was Mr. Berkeley, who arrived in May, 1895. There had been a change of Government in England, and apparently Mr. Berkeley was authorised to alter the policy previously recommended from home. Formal protectorates were established over Unyoro and Usoga, and then over Nandi and Kavirondo.

The condition of Unyoro had been steadily getting worse, and by the end of 1895 Southern Unyoro was in such a deplorable state that Major (then Captain) Pulteney was sent·there to effect a settlement. Pulteney was given wide powers, and he used them well. He made a leading chief, named Rabadongo, chief of

Southern Unyoro, and appointed as his assistants two other chiefs, Makenda and Kikakure. By the aid of these three Wanyoro, Pulteney soon restored order. The natives, trusting to a guarantee that they should not be disturbed so long as they kept quiet, began to recultivate their deserted shambas. They also cut roads, and helped the administration in various ways. The Catholic Waganda, however, objected very strongly to this reinstatement of the Wanyoro in the district that Colvile had given them. They worried Mr. Berkeley until he decided that Pulteney's statesmanlike settlement must be rescinded. Pulteney regarded this decision as a breach of faith with the Wanyoro, and, rather than be concerned in such an act, resigned his position as Civil Officer of Southern Unyoro. He was succeeded by Forster, who was ordered to carry out the new policy, which he was assured was not intended to inflict the slightest practical injustice on individuals. The people were to be persuaded to recognise the supremacy of the Catholic Waganda, but their property and persons were to be unmolested so long as they kept quiet. Rabadongo was removed to Northern Unyoro, and his two assistants were superseded. The natives, however, trusting to promises of protection and safety, stayed in their villages, and the province remained in peace. But then came another change at Kampala. Mr. Berkeley returned to England, and the new Acting Commissioner resolved to allow the Catholic Waganda the full rights they had been granted by Colvile. He gave them the necessary authorization, and they called on the Resident in Unyoro to instal them in possession of some of the land and villages in his district, and compel the native Wanyoro to remain as labourers. This was in defiance of the pledges given the Wanyoro by Forster, and he resigned his post, rather than be the instrument for the enslavement of the Wanyoro by their hereditary foes. Forster was transferred to another district, and the province he had kept in peace broke out into revolt. The British fort and the French Mission were both stormed and destroyed, and the Waganda chiefs promptly chased back to their own country.

Though Unyoro was thus in chaos, in Uganda itself the officials were satisfied with the general outlook, and trusted for great progress from the improved methods of transport to the coast. A bullock road from Mombasa to the Nyanza had been completed, and a steamer was to be at once sent up for service on the lake. The efforts of the Government to place an effective steamer on the Victoria Nyanza have been singularly unlucky. In January, 1895, a sectional steamer of 62 tons was purchased and sent inland by caravans, numbering altogether some 5,000 men. One of the caravans, composed of 1,200 men, was massacred in the Rift Valley by Masai. Many sections of the steamer were lost or abandoned on the road, where they were ruined by rust.

Bishop Tucker met one of the caravans in August, 1895, and found it so reduced by death and disease that he sadly confessed " the prospect of the steamer being at work on the lake within five years is very remote." A new and slightly larger steamer was bought in 1896, and Captain Sclater, the builder of the road to Uganda, was preparing to carry it to the lake in light steel waggons, made for the purpose at Woolwich Arsenal. But this promising young officer died at Zanzibar, a victim to the treacherous East African climate, and the attempts to carry the steamer to the lake were for a time abandoned.

Mr. Berkeley left Uganda in December, 1896, for a visit to England, and Captain (now Major) Ternan was made Acting Commissioner.

At this time Mwanga was feeling especially aggrieved with the British. Some boys whom he ill-treated had been taken from him; he had been recently reminded that he was now only a vassal, and could be easily replaced; and in November, 1896, he was much annoyed by being compelled to pay duty on a transaction in ivory, and at being roughly taken to task for an attempt to evade payment.

The king was therefore secretly hostile to the British; and many of his subjects and subject chiefs had their own private grievances. The Soudanese were very unpopular with the people, as foreign mercenaries in a conquered state generally are. Some of the chiefs had just cause for complaint at acts of oppression by the officers resident in their districts. Thus Kasagama, whom Lugard had reinstated as King of Toru, was so ill-treated by the Resident in his state, that he complained to Kampala; and, as his appeal was supported by Bishop Tucker, an official inquiry was held, and judgment given for Kasagama. But other chiefs, who had less influential supporters, had to nurse their grievances in secret.

The country was, therefore, simmering with discontent, but the leading officials were unconscious of the unpopularity of British rule. On the Commissioner's departure he reported that all was well, and one of the Vice-Consuls wrote that "everything is quiet in Uganda and Unyoro; the people are settling down, and there is not the least likelihood of any trouble with them." The missionaries, however, who were now engaging with most encouraging success in their proper religious and educational work, saw more truly. Archdeacon Walker, one of the ablest of the British missionaries, wrote in July "that the number of natives who hate the missions and all Europeans is very large. They are only restrained from showing open hostility because the Government is too strong for them."

The Catholics also saw that trouble was brewing, and patriotically thrice warned the Government. But the warnings were despised, and Major Ternan led the whole of the efficient Soudanese troops on an expedition against Kamasia, a country some 300 miles east of

UGANDA UNDER THE FOREIGN OFFICE

Uganda. The force devastated Kamasia and also the adjacent country of Nandi. The country of Ketosh was also to have been invaded, but the tribe was saved by the protests of Mr. Grant, who said that it was in his district, and that as the people were innocent of offence they must not be attacked.

The absence of the efficient part of the Soudanese garrison on this seemingly unnecessary expedition gave Mwanga his chance. He fled from the capital on 5th July, 1897, and his departure was the signal for a widespread revolt in Western Uganda. Ternan was recalled, and returned by forced marches to the capital, and thence westward to Budu to quell the revolt.

Ternan drove the enemy from the field. Mwanga escaped, and it looked as if the danger were past. Ternan returned to Kampala, where he received orders to send 300 Soudanese to the Rift Valley as escort of an expedition under Major Macdonald to "the sources of the Juba river."

A new danger was threatening the Uganda Protectorate. The French had for some years been endeavouring to avenge their diplomatic defeats in Egypt by securing political predominance in Abyssinia, and the annexation of the Bahr-el-Ghazl to the French Congo. It is unnecessary to enter into the full details of the policy, but the main principle may be briefly stated.

By various proclamations Egypt, after the fall of Khartum in 1885, had announced her abandonment of her Equatorial Provinces. King John of Abyssinia was persuaded to try to help the escape of the garrisons, and the Emin Pasha Relief Expedition was only the last of a series of efforts made to remove the surviving Egyptian troops. Egypt therefore had officially announced her withdrawal from the Soudan. The British Government had acquiesced in this decision, not only by official approval in 1885 and 1886, but by subsequently treating the Soudanese provinces as derelict, and annexing part of them to the Uganda Protectorate.

Moreover, by the Lisbon Despatch of August, 1887, England had laid down the principle that there was no right of sovereignty in Africa unless supported by effective occupation.

"It has now," says this despatch, "been admitted in principle by all the parties to the Act of Berlin that a claim of sovereignty in Africa can only be maintained by real occupation of the territory claimed." England accordingly, in 1887, sent to Portugal "a formal protest against any claims not founded on occupation."

The French argument was that as Egypt was not in occupation, effective or otherwise, of the Bahr-el-Ghazl, she would have had no rights of ownership there even had she not expressly renounced them.

Moreover, England had annexed part of the Soudanese provinces as the hinterland of Uganda, and had leased another part of them to the Congo Free State (without any reference in the least to the rights of the Khedive). Therefore France maintained that she had the equal right to annex the Bahr-el-Ghazl as the hinterland of the French Congo if she could establish that effective occupation which, according to the British principle, alone gives rights of sovereignty.

Accordingly, M. Liotard, the head of the French State on the Upper Congo, established stations in the former Equatorial Provinces of Egypt on the upper tributaries of the Bahr-el-Ghazl. On this action being unofficially reported England declared that she would consider any such action as unfriendly; but the French declined to be bluffed by this pronouncement, and the Chamber of Deputies publicly voted money for their expeditions in the Bahr-el-Ghazl. The French advanced slowly and steadily, and a force under Major Marchand descended the Bahr-el-Ghazl and established itself at Fashoda on the Nile. It waited there for the arrival of an Abyssinian army which, under French officers, was advancing eastward to occupy the country between Abyssinia and the Nile.

There was no particular secrecy about these expeditions, but the reports as to their progress were discredited in England. At length it could no longer be doubted that the French and Abyssinians were doing their best to establish a French belt across Africa, cutting off any connection between British East Africa and Egypt. Then the Foreign Office took action.

An expedition was organized to advance from the Uganda Road into the territory between Abyssinia and Fashoda, which was admittedly the important strategic district. The Anglo-Italian frontier, to the east of Lake Rudolf, in the upper basin of the Juba River, had not been deliminated; accordingly, it was announced that the expedition was to explore "the sources of the Juba River," a phrase which roused the ire of Mr. Labouchere. The statement was, however, technically true. There is a small river known as the Juba to the north-west of Lake Rudolf, and part of the work of the new expedition was to explore the upper part of this less-known Juba.

The official statement was, however, undeniably misleading, as it was naturally thought to refer to the great Juba River that enters the Indian Ocean at Kismayu. The real destination was soon divulged by a political indiscretion. The instructions and despatches regarding the expedition were carefully edited before publication to prevent the secret being betrayed. But a Blue-Book published part of the despatch which ordered the Acting Commissioner in Uganda to provide a Soudanese escort for the expedition. A sentence was unfortunately left in which

THE UGANDA RAILWAY: SCENERY NEAR VOI STATION.

directed that this escort was to contain as many members as possible of the tribes of the Dinka and Shilluk, that is of the tribes around Fashoda and the Lower Sobat.

After that announcement there could be no doubt that the aim of the "Juba" expedition was to reach Fashoda and the Nile before the French expeditions could arrive, under Marchand from the west and Clochette from the east.

The expedition was the most powerful that had ever been organized in British East Africa. It had a staff of ten European officers, an escort of fifty Sikhs and three hundred Soudanese, and it carried seven Maxims. Its leader was Colonel J. R. L. Macdonald.

The expedition left the coast in detachments during the middle of 1897. The caravan was to be organized and the real start made from a camp to the south of Lake Baringo. Its escort was ordered to join at the Eldoma Ravine, where the road from Uganda descends into the Rift Valley.

The call for a Soudanese escort reached Uganda at an unlucky time. The three efficient companies of Soudanese had been overworked by the expeditions to Kamasia and Budu, and on their return from the latter they were ordered to start at once on a prolonged journey in the country to the north of Uganda.

The three companies selected were taken to the

ravine station by their commandant, Major Ternan, who was proceeding to the coast on his way home. They were transferred to Macdonald, who began his march to the north on 21st September. Two days later they deserted in a body and returned to the Eldoma Ravine station to complain to Mr. Jackson, the Acting Commissioner, of the treatment they had received from their new commander.

So far the act was a matter of insubordination and not of mutiny. The Soudanese apparently had no intentions of mischief, as they allowed the late Captain Kirkpatrick, one of Macdonald's staff, to ride through them on his way to warn the late Lieutenant Fielding, who was in command of the station at the Ravine.

When the first of the Soudanese reached Eldoma they were ordered to lay down their arms and go into the fort. They refused to do anything until the rest of their party had arrived. Captain Kirkpatrick threatened to fire upon them if they persisted in disobedience. The reply was that he might fire. The Maxim gun was brought out, against the protests of Lieutenant Fielding, who, though junior in rank to Captain Kirkpatrick, was senior in East African service and in experience of the Soudanese. His protests were disregarded, and the Maxim was trailed upon the Soudanese and Kirkpatrick gave the order to open fire. The gun, according to the official account, jammed. According to the unofficial account it did not fire from a cause which reflects less discredit on the mechanism of the gun and much credit on the men behind it.

As Kirkpatrick could not shoot down the Soudanese with the Maxim, he ordered the garrison to use their rifles. They could not disobey, but they took care to fire high, and no blood was shed. But the Soudanese were outraged by this reward for their years of loyal service and fled further from the fort.

Next day they were interviewed by Mr. Jackson. The tone of his report suggests that he believed the men's story, and sympathized with their grievances. He had no option whatever but to order the men to return to Macdonald, and the men absolutely refused. After a short delay, the Soudanese marched to a Government stockade at Nandi, eighty miles to the west. They were joined by the garrison, arrested Captain Bagnall, the officer in charge, and looted the station. Then, releasing Bagnall, they marched westward toward Lubwa's, the station on the eastern bank of the Nile, at its outlet from the Victoria Nyanza.

The station at Lubwa's had a small Soudanese garrison, under an officer named Wilson. When the news of the mutiny reached Uganda, Major Thruston, the commandant of the Uganda Rifles, chivalrously started for Lubwa's to secure the loyalty of its garrison, and persuade the mutineers to return to duty.

He reached Lubwa's on October 4th. The garrison

swore loyalty to him; he sent a message to the Soudanese urging them to return to their allegiance, and promising that they should not be forced to serve under Macdonald. But on the night of October the 16th the mutineers reached the fort. The garrison were irritated by the arrest of some of their women in Uganda, and they admitted the mutineers. Thruston and Wilson were seized and put in chains. Next day a third European prisoner was taken, as the Government's steam launch ran up to the fort, and its engineer, Scott, did not know that the mutineers were in possession.

The same day Macdonald's force arrived in pursuit, and took up a station on the hill opposite Lubwa's. Thruston sent Macdonald a characteristically chivalrous letter, asking him not to fight unless attacked, but not to let any considerations for his own safety interfere with the plans for the suppression of the mutiny.

Early next day (October 19th) three hundred of the mutineers left Lubwa's to have a "shauri" with Macdonald. They advanced in irregular order, laughing and talking until they were fifty yards from the camp. Macdonald tells us that they then treacherously opened fire. There is some doubt as to this fact. The method of the Soudanese advance does not look much like an intended surprise attack. But a gun went off on one side or the other. Both sides appear to have suspected that the other was beginning a treacherous attack, and the firing became general. After a severe fight, in which Lieutenant Fielding and Lieutenant Macdonald were killed, and Mr. Jackson severely wounded, the mutineers were driven back with heavy loss, including Mabruk Effendi, one of the two leaders of the mutiny.

In the afternoon two of the Soudanese went as a deputation to Macdonald to ask for terms. They were ordered to surrender unconditionally. Though they had now three European prisoners in their hands, they were offered the same terms as at the ravine, when the worst punishment they had to fear was for an act of petulant insubordination. The Soudanese were infuriated at this reply. It may have been that their officers were anxious to prevent the men from surrendering by inciting them to a step which would cut off all hopes of mercy. The three Englishmen were brought from the guard hut, and told that they were to be shot. Thruston insisted that, if he were to be shot it must be by the Soudanese commander, Bilal Effendi. Bilal accordingly raised his rifle. Thruston fearlessly caught hold of the muzzle and held it against his forehead. A moment later he fell, shot through the head. Wilson and Scott were led away and shot in the back.

This terrible outrage rendered further negotiations useless, and the siege of Lubwa's was begun by Macdonald, aided by a large force of the Waganda. Meanwhile the news of the Soudanese revolt had spread through Uganda, and the Waganda again rose in rebellion. Fortunately, most of the other Soudanese troops, who had not the same grievances as the three companies that mutinied, remained loyal; but, as a precautionary measure, they were ordered to lay down their arms, and they promptly obeyed. But without the services of the Soudanese troops the Waganda rebels could not be easily kept in check. For some time the position at Kampala was critical.

Luckily, the Acting Commissioner at this time was Mr. George Wilson, who had been in British East Africa ever since 1889. He is a man remarkable for the keen personal interest he takes in the natives, and for his infinite patience in dealing with them. He has a wide command of East African languages, and will spend hours in conversation with a party of natives, without betraying boredom or impatience. His knowledge of the character of the natives is intimate, and his power with them is great.

Thanks in the main to the influence of Wilson and Grant, and to the loyal assistance given by the two missionary parties, further disasters were averted and the country held, until the arrival of reinforcements from the coast.

Meanwhile the mutineers were still besieged at Lubwa's. An attempt to storm the fort on October 28th was repulsed with severe loss, and the garrison held its own until the beginning of January, 1897, when they escaped across the bay, and marched northwards down the Nile. They occupied a fresh position at Lake Kioga, where they were attacked and defeated. The British forces were now reinforced by Indian troops, and the Soudanese were overwhelmed. They fought bravely, but after a series of stubborn engagements, fought with varying success, they were finally crushed and scattered.

The Soudanese mutiny is the saddest of the many sad stories in the recent history of Uganda. It necessitated the destruction of the loyal garrison that had held Uganda for England. It involved a deplorable waste of valuable European life, and gave the Waganda the opportunity of renewing their rebellion. The cost of its suppression was enormous, and the loss to the country through civil war and devastation has ruined native trade or diverted it to routes outside the British sphere. Economically and politically the harm has been irreparable. And the pity of it is that the Soudanese deserve sympathy rather than blame. They were the victims of intolerable grievances, and were driven to rebellion by tactless treatment.

The blame for the mutiny is not to be charged against any one man. It was due to several causes, and Macdonald's quarrel with his men at the ravine was only the irritant that caused the bursting of the bonds of discipline, strained by a long course of ill-treatment.

The Soudanese had just cause for disaffection. Their

pay was miserably inadequate. The Zanzibari porters, upon whom the Soudanese looked down with contempt, had a pay of ten rupees a month. The Soudanese in the Uganda Protectorate received only four rupees a month. When they reached Eldoma, they found that the Soudanese in the pay of the adjacent Coast Protectorate, though men of the same race, and acting in corresponding positions, were receiving more than six times as much pay, viz., twenty-six rupees a month.

What is still more discreditable is that even the stingy pittance of four rupees a month was often not paid for months after it was due. It is barely credible that the pay of the Soudanese in Uganda should have been sometimes six months in arrears, but the evidence is conclusive. It is true that the men's wages were paid in cloth, which cannot be remitted by the ordinary financial methods. But this excuse for the Turkish irregularity in pay is not sufficient, as some East Coast firms had offered to transport to Uganda as many loads as were required. Their proposals were declined, though the Government transport service was admittedly inefficient.

The consequences of the irregularity in the payment of the Soudanese were unfortunate. As polygamous Mohammedans, most of the Soudanese had several wives and large families. When they did not get their wages, they could not buy any food. It was not to be expected that they would stand by and see their families starve in a land of plenty. So of course they stole food from the natives. The Waganda bitterly resented the thefts, and the feud between the natives and our mercenaries increased the unpopularity of our rule.

Another grievance of the three companies that rebelled (the 4th, 7th, and 9th) was the fact that they were steadily overworked, while other companies were allowed to live at ease as garrisons in stations. These three companies had been drilled and trained by Major Cunningham, who did his work well. Hence, whenever there was fighting to be done, it was less trouble to send the three trained companies rather than break in the others. This was particularly unfair in the case of the Soudanese troops, because they had been allowed small grants of land as gardens to help them in the support of their families. While they were kept continually on the march, they had no time to till their allotments, and the grants were useless.

The Soudanese, moreover, appear to have been tactlessly and unsympathetically handled by some of their British officers. To men like Gibb and Thruston, who knew their language and understood their nature, the Soudanese were devoted, until they were maddened to anger and despair. But they complained bitterly of their treatment by the young and inexperienced officers sent out to command them, who did not know their language and would not listen to their complaints. In the latter part of Major Ternan's command he had inflicted punishments on two companies which they bitterly resented. In Bilal Effendi's company (the 9th) all the non-commissioned officers were degraded a step, because they demanded their arrears of pay. In the company of Mabruk Effendi, the second leader of the mutiny, the officers and sergeants were all reduced in rank because they refused, from their hereditary terror of witchcraft, to arrest a native who was accused of having bewitched one of the men.

It was while the men were thus dissatisfied by overwork, irregularity in the payment of their scanty wage, and tactless treatment by some of their officers that Ternan was ordered to send 300 Soudanese as escort to Macdonald's expedition. Companies 4, 7, and 9 were as usual selected.

They reached the ravine, smarting under a sense of injustice for their treatment in the past, and they were prejudiced against their future commander, for apparently some, at least, of the Soudanese had not forgotten or forgiven Macdonald's treatment of Selim Bey in 1893. Opinions differ as to how far this factor helped in the outbreak. But it is stated that Bilal Effendi, before leaving Uganda, swore on the head of his son, one of the most solemn of Mohammedan oaths, that he would never serve again under Macdonald; and the telegram from the Acting Consul-General at Zanzibar, which announced the mutiny, states that the Soudanese declared, "they did not care for constant expeditions, particularly those of Major Macdonald."

As soon as the men were transferred to their new commander the trouble began. The Soudanese, knowing how they were hated by the Waganda, asked for some assurances that their women should be properly protected during their absence. They also asked that some of the women might be allowed to accompany them. Both requests were reasonable. The Soudanese are generally attended in a campaign by their wives, who light fires, cook food, build grass huts, tie up loads, and do other work which the soldiers regard as menial or for which they have no time. This system is so regular that the Foreign Office had arranged for some of the women to be sent on the expedition, but the men had not been informed of it. The men, on joining Macdonald's expedition, asked for a shauri or conference in which to state their grievances. Macdonald refused to see them, but told one of the native officers, Mabruk Effendi, what arrangements had been made. There was either some misunderstanding over Macdonald's assurances, or Mabruk deliberately suppressed the message. The latter, however, is improbable, as any such treacherous action would have been inevitably discovered at the conference which the men, with Mabruk's approval, demanded for the next day. On the following morning the men drew up in line ready to march north with part of the caravan. According to the men's account, as reported by Jackson, the men, through their commandant, Lieutenant Bright, begged for an interview with Macdonald. He walked toward them, and the men expected some explanations and assurances. Instead of that they were brusquely ordered to "Right turn, quick march." The men looked appealingly to Lieutenant Bright, and asked, "What is the meaning of this? We want to see him; he comes and won't speak to us, but orders us away. We won't go, but will run away."

The Soudanese accordingly fled to complain to Jackson. Apparently they thought that if they were to be treated thus at the first camp, what might they not expect when they got far away from Uganda into the deserts to the north?

The impolicy of this unsympathetic treatment of the Soudanese request for information may be judged by Stanley's speech on the mutiny in the House of Commons. The instructions issued by the Foreign Office for the conduct of the expedition ordered that the native tribes met with were to be treated with consideration and respect. If, said Stanley after quoting that order, the commander had also been instructed to treat his own escort with consideration and respect, there would have been no Soudanese mutiny. Uganda would have been spared the most disastrous period in the last decade of its history.

Chapter XIII

THE FUTURE OF BRITISH EAST AFRICA

"Wherefore such persons as be illuminated with the brightest irradiations of knowledge and of the veritie and due proportion of things, they are called by the learned men not *phantastici* but *euphantasiote*, and of this sort of phantasie are all good Poets, notable Captaines strategematique, all cunning artificers and engineers, all Legislators, Politiciens, and Counsellours of estate, in whose exercises the inventive part is most employed, and is to the sound judgement of man most needful."

—George Puttenham, 1589.

WHEN in 1893 the British Government decided to relieve the Chartered Company of its work in British East Africa, high hopes were formed of a great commercial prosperity for the country. Our new protectorate was generally believed to be of great economic value. The land, with its vast areas of rich volcanic soil, was described as of the highest agricultural capabilities. It was expected to yield rich harvests of rubber, fibre, coffee, cotton, and oils, as well as sufficient food stuffs to support a dense population. The ivory trade was important and lucrative, and was carried on by many native caravans. Silver had been found a few miles from Mombasa; a rock that looked like quartz was abundant, and some out-crops of it had been described on the maps as "quartz very likely looking for gold." Gold itself had been collected in the nepheline syenite of Mount Jombo, south of Mombasa, and near this locality ought to occur alluvial deposits that would pay local working.

Warnings that East Africa might be poorer than was expected were uttered. Scott Elliot, for example, says, in reference to the Nyika, that "the general impression of the country is very bad, and its commercial future probably means only the formation of perhaps twenty ostrich farms. One can only buy a chicken at four places between Mombasa and Kibwezi"—a distance of 190 miles. But the general estimate of the economic value of British East Africa is shown in a series of opinions collected by Lugard, who concludes that "East Africa is not an El Dorado, but the testimony of all the authorities I have quoted is unanimous as to the fertility of the soil, the healthiness of the highlands, the abundance of the rainfall, and the general excellence of the climate."

Mr. W. A. Fitzgerald, who travelled through the districts near the coast as expert botanical adviser to the British East Africa Company, reports that, for fifty miles into the interior "the country is, as a whole, exceedingly rich and fertile, there can be no possible doubt ; in the coast-lands, especially, we possess an extent of territory which for productiveness and richness of soil it would be difficult to equal, whilst in the extensive forests along the banks of the Sabaki there are possibilities of future wealth and prosperity which only require development to be realized."

Fitzgerald's opinion was formed after a study of the coast-lands, and some of the inland provinces were believed to be still more valuable.

Uganda, in particular, was regarded as a land of great commercial importance, and the urgent demand for its annexation by the British Chambers of Commerce testifies to the high estimate of its economic value. German East Africa was described as poor in contrast. Thus, Dr. Hans Meyer admits that "in East Africa England has decidedly had the best of the bargain. In Uganda she possesses at once the most highly cultivated and the most densely populated region in Equatorial Africa, and the key to the Soudan and Egypt."

Uganda being thus regarded as the commercial "pearl of Africa," it was necessary to bring it into direct communication with the coast. As the East African rivers are of little value for transport, a railway was said to be the prime necessity of British East Africa.

A preliminary railway survey was made in 1892-3 under the superintendence of Major Macdonald, who estimated that the railway from Mombasa to the Victoria Nyanza would be 657 miles long, and for a

3 ft. 6 in. gauge would cost £2,240,000. The interest on this sum would amount to £66,000 a year, and there would be at first a loss on working expenses of £4,000 a year (Report on Mombasa—Victoria Lake Railway Survey Parl. Pap., 1893, C. 7025, p. 27). It was estimated that transport from the interior would pay for articles that could afford ·4*d*. per ton-mile rate, or 22*s*. a ton from the lake to the coast. Hence, for a moderate liability of £70,000 a year, a railway could be laid from the coast to the lake. It was predicted that with these facilities for transport a trade would soon develop, sufficient to pay for the administration of the country.

The railway was begun in 1895, and is still in progress. It is under the management of a Foreign Office Committee, of which the chairman was Sir Percy Anderson, succeeded after his death in 1896 by Sir Francis Bertie and Sir Clement Hill; Mr. George Whitehouse was appointed local engineer, and Sir L. O'Callaghan the managing director in London. Fresh surveys reduced the length of line required to 550 miles, and, to further lower the cost, the gauge was reduced to a metre. But this year (1900), in addition to the original vote of £3,000,000, which is £760,000 (or a third) more than Macdonald's estimate, an extra £1,930,000 has been voted for the work.

The railway has already been voted more than twice as much as the first estimate, and it will probably cost

THE UGANDA RAILWAY : CLEARING FOR MOMBASA STATION.

THE FUTURE OF BRITISH EAST AFRICA

still more before it is finished. Though it is a wild exaggeration to describe it as "the English Panama," it is hopeless to expect it to pay interest on its capital. But if, as may reasonably be expected, it pays its working expenses, its construction will have been justified, as it was built for political reasons, and not as a commercial speculation.

Whether the Uganda Railway will be a success, the future alone can decide. But the character of the British Imperial administration in British East Africa is a topic fairly open to discussion, for there are six years' results on which to base an opinion.

The rule of the Foreign Office has been accompanied by great progress, for most of which the Foreign Office and its East African staff deserve the credit.

Mombasa from an Arab town has become a Europeanized commercial city; roads have been built; transport improved; the railway has been steadily pushed inland, and towns have grown up beside it; some of the most turbulent tribes have been overawed by the establishment of forts in their districts; the Pokomo of the Tana have received protection from the raids of the Masai and Somali; the Wakamba have learnt to appreciate the benefits of European government, and to assist with reliable work. Nevertheless, it must be admitted that the great expectations of 1894 have not been fulfilled. The progress of the country has been very partial. The volume of external trade has increased, owing to the influx of railway officials and the import of railway plant. But the natural trade has not grown; old trade routes have been abandoned and native markets closed; land has gone out of cultivation; pestilence and famine have swept through the country, and the population has been reduced by war, disease, and emigration.

The results have been most disappointing to those who hailed the establishment of Imperial rule as a guarantee that East Africa would soon enjoy a better peace than she has ever known. The disappointment has been all the more bitter as there has been a heavy loss of valuable European life, and the failures have occurred in spite of the noblest and self-sacrificing efforts of a devoted band of officials.

The causes of the disappointing results of the British rule are not far to seek. They are painfully obvious. The whole of the blame does not rest with man. Some of the worst faults lie in the structure of the universe. British East Africa is, and must always be, a troublesome country to rule, and the geographical conditions render its government, from a distant office on second-hand knowledge of its needs, exceptionally difficult.

The first estimates of the value of the country were far too optimistic. Colonel Pearson, in his despatches on the campaign against the rebel Mazrui, tells us that "the physical difficulties offered by the country

THE FUTURE OF BRITISH EAST AFRICA

to the movement of troops are far beyond any that have been recorded ot expeditions in India. The blistering force of the sun, the stifling heat of the jungles, and the scarcity of water, render operations in the lowlands near the coast extremely arduous and trying."

Moreover, during the last six years British East Africa has had persistent ill-luck. Pestilence, drought, and famine are enemies that, in a comparatively unknown land, can neither be foreseen nor controlled; and they have devastated British East Africa, and engendered widespread misery and a spirit of unrest that have caused especial irritation against civilized restraint.

But the blame for the confusion in British East Africa is not all extra-human. The clumsiness of man and the conservatism of government systems have been only too powerful for evil. Rebellion is only too easily roused among people so governed by habit and so saturated with superstition as negroes, when their rulers fail to realize the spiritual basis of fetish worship and despise reverence for blocks of wood and stone as mere heathen folly. It is not difficult to point out blunders after they have been advertised by their results, and to grumble at acts of impatience committed by men perhaps suffering from a burning fever or abscessed livers in a hot and unhealthy climate. Lord Curzon once eloquently expressed his surprise that men working under such trying conditions as our Uganda staff have not committed more and greater blunders. And no one can read the history of British East Africa without the highest admiration for the work of European officials. England has been represented in East Africa by men who have worked there in accordance with the best traditions of our colonial policy. Thus amongst the administrators there have been George S. Mackenzie and J. R. W. Piggott, both of whom by tact and sympathy secured the goodwill of the leading Arabs during the rule of the British East Africa Company; and Sir A. Hardinge, whose intimate knowledge of Arab character has enabled him to reconcile the planters of Zanzibar and Pemba to our anti-slavery legislation. There have been model district administrators, such as Ainsworth of Machakos, Hobley in Kavirondo, Hall in Kikuyu, Grant in Usogo, and Forster in Unyoro. Confidence in British justice has been established by Jenner's[1] integrity and impartiality as Chief Judge at Mombasa. Men, such as Bird Thompson at Witu, Pulteney in Unyoro, Rogers at Lamu, Sitwell in Toru, Cunningham and Gibb in Uganda, though in military commands, have restrained their natural instinct for fighting and have worked with single-souled devotion and untiring patience at the peaceful administration of

[1] The sad news that Jenner was killed by the southern Somali was received after this chapter was in type.

THE FUTURE OF BRITISH EAST AFRICA

their districts. Finally, men like George Wilson and F. J. Jackson, owing to their sympathy with the natives, have been able to carry the country through crises in its history.

To mention individuals is no doubt invidious; the men named are but samples of the rest. It is the fact that the majority of the British East African staff have worked sincerely and disinterestedly for the welfare of the country, that makes so deplorable the frequent waste of their sacrifices by the clumsiness of inexperienced colleagues and the adoption of official methods unsuited to local conditions.

The main cause of our disasters in the rule of the Foreign Office, as in that of its predecessor, the British East Africa Company, has been the lack of a policy based on a scientific knowledge of the country and its people, framed in accordance with the views of the local authorities as to what is practically and economically possible, and continuously and consistently carried out, even despite the prejudices of philanthropists at home and the ambitions of military officials abroad.

The British East Africa Company was ruined by the attempt suddenly to introduce a government, on philanthropic principles, into a country too poor to afford a sudden revolution of its industrial system, and to pay for the luxury of social experiments.

The policy enforced from home by the Company was of extraneous origin, and the climate of East

Africa was fatal to it. The main fault of the Foreign Office rule has been exactly the reverse: either it has not had any consistent policy or ideal of its own, or it has failed to insist on the adoption of that policy by its agents in East Africa. There has been a rapid succession of Commissioners and Acting Commissioners, who have been allowed to do what they wanted, whether or not it was consistent with the acts of their predecessors or the views of the Government.

Since 1893 Uganda has been governed successively by Portal, Macdonald, Colvile, Jackson, Berkeley, Ternan, Jackson, Wilson, Berkeley, and finally Sir Harry Johnston. The changes of policy with these changes of men have been sudden and complete. Portal's system, of a minimum interference in local administration and peace with neighbouring states, was promptly reversed by his successor. An adventurous policy has naturally been more popular in Uganda, for it has been better rewarded at home than attempts at the quiet development of the country. The man, who made successfully one of those "nigger hunts," which in Equatorial Africa are misnamed wars, has gained distinction and decoration, in preference to the man who kept his province in peace by sympathetic and patient administration. The Chinese system of paying a doctor most when he attends his patient least might well be adopted for rewarding soldiers who have civilian duties. Some of the wars and punitive

THE FUTURE OF BRITISH EAST AFRICA

expeditions of the past few years have been no doubt inevitable and just. They have been "the cruel wars of peace." But some of the military expeditions in East Africa have been simply criminal in their folly and thoughtlessness.

In one instance a village of a chief, with whom it was especially necessary that friendly relations should be maintained, was attacked and looted by an officer on his way home from Uganda out of sheer mischief. Once on a time the chief had been troublesome, but he had been cajoled into good behaviour by the tactful handling of the officer in command of the district; and his work of years was undone in an afternoon by the caprice of an irresponsible officer from a distant province.

Acts such as these not only shatter the confidence of the natives, but they dishearten the men whose work is thus lightly ruined.

Some of the incidents that have attended British conquests of fractious tribes have been perfectly horrible, as is admitted by the men who were forced to commit them. Thruston's interesting memoir tells us of several which occurred during the campaign that ruined the once fertile and well-peopled country of Unyoro. Thruston relates that, during a night march on Kabarega's stronghold in 1894, he passed a hut with three men sitting inside it smoking. "It was impossible that we could pass without being discovered, so I stopped, and, turning round, made a sign to the soldiers. As I did so, one of the men got up and went towards the door. But the soldiers had understood me well; they had fixed their bayonets. In a moment a dozen of them had run into the house and silently done their work. This transaction, I know, comes very near to mere assassination."

Thruston describes his duty in Unyoro as that of "a captain of Bashi-Bazouks, a raider, and an ivory thief"; and he complains, "I was sick of raids and bloodshed, and I longed to have done with them." He therefore wrote to Kabarega, the king of the country, to beg him to submit. But Thruston tells us that "this letter was promptly repudiated by the Foreign Office," and endorses the opinion expressed by Mr. Byles in the House of Commons, that every one who had been in any way connected with Unyoro ought to be thoroughly ashamed of himself—a condemnation which Thruston candidly accepted for himself.

The work of civilian administration in East Africa has also been seriously hindered by the quarrels of the missions and their interference in politics. The difficulty thus introduced into the government of Uganda has been admitted by every independent visitor to the country.

I have had to criticise the missionaries in Chapter

Photo by]   [*Gomes, Zanzibar.*
THE UGANDA RAILWAY: A STEEP GRADIENT.

XI., and should like to remark that I have no animus against them. I had taken a keen interest in mission work, and went to East Africa in full sympathy with it. I realized that the missionaries are the one section of Europeans in an uncivilized community whose interests are one with the natives, whom they best can protect against ill-treatment by traders or officials.[1] The missions in East Africa have done work which every student of that country must admire, from its untiring patience, its educational success as at Freretown, and the extent of its civilizing influence as in Uganda. The East African Mission has on its roll the names of men of saintly life and of Christian spirit, like Krapf and Rebmann of the old Mombasa Mission, Mackay and Tucker of Uganda, Hooper of Jelori, Smith and Edwards of Freretown, and W. E. Taylor of Mombasa. But the work of these men has been hampered by the political interference of the missionaries as a body. Missionary intervention in politics has been as disastrous in Eastern Africa as it has been in other parts of the continent.

The effort of the London Missionary Society's agents to make South Africa into a group of native states ruled by local chiefs, under the guidance of missionary advisers, was one great cause of the feud at the Cape between the English and the Dutch settlers. In

[1] As in the case of Bishop Tucker's excellent intervention in Toru, p. 179.

Uganda, in the British East African coast-lands, and in British Central Africa, the political action of the missionaries has done deplorable harm to the countries, to the missions, and to the missionaries. It would no doubt often have been difficult for the missionaries to avoid intervention; but some of them seem to have been only too willing to exchange preaching for the excitement of political intrigue.

A minute of the Church Missionary Society declares that "one of the fundamental principles of the Society is that the committee and missionaries must keep clear of politics." This rule may be obeyed in Asia, but in Uganda it has many a time been absolutely neglected. Indeed, Sir Gerald Portal asserted that the race for converts in Uganda was synonymous with a race for political power. Now, however, there can be no doubt about the future ownership of Uganda; so we may hope that the Church Missionary Society will enforce its own wise rule, that its agents are not to interfere in political affairs. Until the missionaries are persuaded to work on this principle, it is idle to expect African natives to believe that missions are solely inspired by religious motives.

A second change that is wanted is more tolerance for rival missions. That the bitter feud between the Catholics and Protestants in Uganda has been the great difficulty in ruling that country has been recognised by every independent visitor. The bitterness between the

THE FUTURE OF BRITISH EAST AFRICA 251

two parties can be best illustrated by extracts from the writings of the missionaries themselves. The diary of the French Mission in Uganda is printed in the official *Chronique Trimestrielle de la Société des Missionaires d'Afrique* (*Pères-Blancs*). This journal, which is now in its twenty-first year, is especially instructive, as it is not issued for general circulation. A notice, printed on both leaves of the cover, reminds all whom it may concern that the *Chronique Trimestrielle*, being published exclusively for the Missionary Fathers, ought not to be communicated to any other person whatever without the permission of the "Supérieurs majeurs." Care is taken to prevent the journal falling into the hands of what it calls "Protestant pagans"; but copies are occasionally read by others than the White Fathers, and a few quotations will illustrate the spirit in which some members of the Catholic Mission conduct their work. The two mottoes of the order are the texts, "Behold, how good and how pleasant it is for brethren to dwell together in unity," and "It [the multitude of them that believed] was of one heart and one soul." How the missionaries interpret these maxims is shown by the following passages, all of which are taken from one number of the *Chronique Trimestrielle* :—

"What a pity that at Rubaga [the headquarters of the French Mission] there is not a missionary specially charged with the conversion of the Protestants." Any such arrangement is unnecessary, since it appears from the diary that the whole staff are ready to devote their best energies to this branch of the work. A few pages earlier is the following passage, " Three teachers armed with a letter from Mwanga leave for Budu to build a church there and introduce heresy into our beloved province. The progress and success of Catholicism in the Protestant provinces make the heretics hope for similar results in Budu. But they will try in vain; for one proselyte neophyte they may make from us, we will glean a hundred from them." The enthusiasm with which the conversion of Protestants is undertaken is illustrated by a remark on the next page. " January 30th. Departure of Fathers Gaudibert and Jacquet for Bulamwezi. Their baggage is light, but they are as gay as larks—they are going to evangelize a Protestant province." Mr. Wilson, the Acting Commissioner at Kampala, had occasion to protest to the king against some of Father Gaudibert's proceedings during the course of this evangelical tour. The complaint is repeated in the journal as follows, with a characteristic comment, "' He [Father Gaudibert] does harm in Bulamwezi; he has many houses built by force. The whites of Namirembe [the headquarters of the Church Missionary Society in Uganda] have denounced him to me.' Bravo, Father Gaudibert. Mr. Wilson pays you a compliment to-day. The Protestants curse you. That proves that you do good, and what are these houses, which cause you to be detested by the chiefs of

THE FUTURE OF BRITISH EAST AFRICA 253

Kampala and the Reverends, but chapels wherein you collect your catechumens, more numerous every day, converted from Protestantism?" A week later Father Gaudibert returned to the French central station, rejoicing in the salvation of "a joyful band of neophytes and catechumens torn from Protestantism. This is the wheat that with the help of God he has known how to glean in the midst of thistles." "During the two past months nine chapels have been built in the midst of the Protestant provinces at the instigation of the catechists and with the help of the catechumens. But in the midst of what broils, what cries of rage from the Protestants? God alone knows. May the Blessed Virgin continue her protection and give us courage in our militant life."

Zeal on the part of the Protestant agents is attributed to inspiration from a different source. "Thousands of printed leaflets are circulating in the capital of Uganda; men posted at every street corner distribute them to the passers-by. It is Pilkington, the crack-brained (*exalté*) minister of Namirembe, who writes a collective letter to all the Buganda from England. This minister, who during his sojourn in Uganda had all the symptoms of diabolical possession, speaks in this letter of his laborious scriptural works — six books were already printed, and others in preparation, with which he will not delay inundating the country."

The Catholic converts, however, are not always gained

by the methods of the Church militant. The following entry shows that recruits are obtained by purchase as well as by preaching, "April 20th. A woman escapes from her Mussulman master, and entreats me to buy her. Four years ago she began to pray daily, morning and evening, and she has been faithful to her prayers, in spite of being forbidden and bastinadoed by her master, she has had herself secretly instructed in the catechism, which she knows by heart. The Mussulman, despairing of corrupting her, has resolved to sell her to a pagan. I buy this poor soul for 5,500 cowries." Father Gaudibert's method of arguing with heretics he describes as follows:—

"About ten o'clock in the morning a *grand diable* of a negro, whose body is all covered with horrid sores, presents himself to me. I have seldom seen a man of so repulsive an aspect. His hideous face, stupefied by abuse of mwenge [native beer], presents to the frightened gaze two eyes terribly reddened by smoking hemp.

"'Where do you come from?'

"'I come from Namirembe [the Church Missionary Society's headquarters]. The whites have sent me here to carry greetings to the lost children of the house of God.'

"'But these reverend gentlemen have not told you to come to me, I think?'

"'They told me to go everywhere, and have fear of no one. But if I had not convinced the Pope's white man of error, people would refuse the greeting I bring.'

"'No, my dear friend, they could not refuse greetings presented by so distinguished a man. Are not your hemp-reddened eyes and the infectious odour that is exhaled by your legs enough to unite round you all the Buganda?'

"'Laugh at me, but listen!'

"'I am not laughing; I am telling the truth pure and simple.'

"'This is what the Lord sends me to tell you.'

"'Wait a minute; what is your name?'

"'My name is Eliya; on this earth my master is Mugema, but in truth I have no other master than that one who says, "There is only one Master," and who has written the evangel I hold in my hand, and which leaves me neither night nor day.'

"'Take care not to dirty it with the pus which flows from your body.'

"'The Lord sends me to tell you that you are a liar. The day of judgment draws near; yet a little while——

"'I a liar? Thanks for your politeness; but tell me why I'm a liar.'

"'Yes, you are a liar, because you teach that Peter is the vicar of Jesus Christ. Open the evangel. Would our Lord Jesus Christ have entrusted His Holy (*sic*) Mother to John if Peter had been His vicar? Would the apostles united at Jerusalem have sent Peter into Samaria if Peter had been their chief? Would Jesus have rebuffed Peter as He did (St. John xxi. 20–23) if He had wished that Peter should be His vicar?' etc., etc.

"I answer all these old objections very seriously to edify the catechumens present, and excite their laughter against this inspired man, whom I would willingly call Pilkingtonian. He, in fact, recalls very well a fool I once knew at the capital. That visionary pretended to have received the Holy Spirit in the island of Kome, and wished to communicate it to every one, whether they wished or not. What an assault I had to endure as my share! Briefly, my good negro, finding it impossible to continue the argument, avowed himself vanquished and changed his weapons. He passed from insolent discussion to downright insult.

"'You white man of Kasala, and all belonging to you, you deceive your people, you teach that the Pope is God.'

"'I teach that the Pope is God?'

"'Yes, you.'

"'Well, as you are so ill-informed, go and ask those whom I teach what is my doctrine.' And, saying this, I show him the door. My demoniac refusing to go, I am obliged to take him by the arm and put him outside. I have all the trouble in the world to prevent my people accompanying this by blows.

"'It is the Lord you are driving away,' he cries, like one possessed; 'The day of judgment is near.'"

This, it must be remembered, is Père Gaudibert's

THE FUTURE OF BRITISH EAST AFRICA

own account of how he spreads the gospel of Christ among the Waganda. It is distressing enough that any native on visiting a Christian mission station should be reviled and ridiculed and then forcibly expelled. But it is worse that the missionary should describe the incident with manifest pleasure and without the slightest feeling of shame. It is still more deplorable that such a narrative should be circulated by the authorities of the Order of the White Fathers among their other stations, apparently as an instance of commendable zeal.

Further, it is to be hoped that the missionaries will become not only more tolerant towards one another, but more patient in demanding reforms of local institutions.

Slavery, when it involved slave-raiding in Africa, a Transatlantic voyage in a crowded slave ship, and work under the harsh discipline of an American plantation, deserved every epithet that its opponents hurled against it. But this type of slavery has disappeared from British East Africa. What is there called slavery is a feudal system which is freedom itself compared with the rigid rules and imprisonment of a South African mining compound. The agitation, in favour of the immediate abolition of East African serfdom owes its strength to feelings that have survived from the crusade of Clarkson and Wilberforce

Even thirty years ago some missionaries admitted that the evils of domestic slavery in East Africa had been exaggerated. In 1873 Rev. C. New objected to the transportation of the freed slaves to the settlements established for them in Mauritius, the Seychelles, Bombay and Aden, because in those places the slaves had to live under discipline and learn various uncongenial subjects—a lot which they regarded as slavery under a less sympathetic and stronger master than they would otherwise have had. "From personal intercourse," says New, "I found that these freed people feel their exile more than they did their original slavery."

That the abuses of domestic serfdom are now insignificant is obvious from the difficulty found by the anti-slavery advocates in discovering sensational scandals. The Anti-slavery Society has been misled into using bogus evidence. In September, 1896, it published in its organ, *The Anti-slavery Reporter*, a photograph of some men in chains, under the title "Slavery in Zanzibar." The picture was re-published in a pamphlet in 1897, when it was described as "A group of slaves under the British flag, Zanzibar," and "Slavery in Zanzibar, 1896." The photograph in reality was an old photograph showing a German soldier guarding some prisoners at Dar-es-Salaam in German East Africa.

If the Society, in spite of its enterprising agents

THE FUTURE OF BRITISH EAST AFRICA

in British East Africa, has to use such evidence as this, the existing evils cannot be extensive. Nevertheless the British public has failed to recognise the difference between the slavery of the American sugar plantations and the domestic serfdom of East Africa. It has, accordingly, forced the British Government to impose on the East African coast-lands labour reforms for which the people were not ready. The effect has therefore been disastrous.

The Germans have been wiser. They began an equally vigorous campaign against slavery. The German Anti-slavery Committee was nothing behind the British Anti-slavery Society in the vigour of its denunciations of slavery and in its efforts to destroy it. But the German administrators soon realized the harm that would result from precipitate interference with domestic serfdom, and they were allowed to proceed slowly. Hence, though they started work in the face of a stronger native prejudice than we did, they have managed to rule their territories without any such serious rebellions as those of Uganda and the Mazrui, which have done such irreparable harm in British East Africa.

So far this chapter has been merely critical. What suggestions, it may be asked, can be made to improve our administrative methods, so as to avoid evils and injustice in the future?

The crying need of East Africa is consistent administration by men who know the country and understand its people. The present Commissioner is the first ruler sent out with full powers who has had considerable experience of the Bantu races. If Sir Harry Johnston had only been sent out five years earlier, how different the story of British East Africa might have been! If his appointment means that there is to be a new system in the selection of officials, then his administration marks the beginning of a brighter era in East Africa.

A radical reform is also necessary in the method of filling the subordinate appointments.

At present British East Africa is governed by the Foreign Office. The qualifications required in diplomatic and consular work are not those wanted for the management of equatorial railways and the government of uncivilized tribes of negroes. The Foreign Office has a staff which has been trained for diplomatic and consular work; but it has no body of men at its disposal who understand the conditions of Equatorial Africa, and who are at the same time available for appointments in East Africa. The Foreign Office has to borrow the services of soldiers, who have learnt to love the formal discipline of European armies, and will even expect native levies to show the self-restraint of British troops. In cases of emergency, the Foreign Office calls for help from India; and, though some

THE FUTURE OF BRITISH EAST AFRICA

of the men of Indian training have achieved brilliant success, others appear to have tried ruling excitable "Fuzzy-Wuzzies" and turbulent Masai as if they were Bengali. The consequences have been tragic.

The primary need of our possessions in Equatorial Africa is a special service of men appointed by open competition, as in the Indian Civil Service. According to the present system, the selection of men is necessarily somewhat haphazard. A man is sent for a few years' work to East Africa; thence he is promoted to act as consul at a Mediterranean watering place or an American port. Aware that promotion may at any time lead to his sudden removal to another continent, he has no particular inducement to take much interest in the country or its people. As soon as a man begins to understand the natives and speak their language, he may be transferred. Similarly, a young official in British East Africa may at any time have placed over his head a man who knows nothing of Africa or African methods, and may do serious mischief before he learns to take advice from his more experienced juniors.

A special service for tropical Africa is needed, not only for the good of our African possessions, but in the interests of the normal work of the Foreign Office. Berths in other parts of the world have to be found for men who have earned promotion in Equatorial Africa. The most striking illustration of the disadvantages of this system is the case of Sir Claude Macdonald, who made a great reputation by the high character and brilliant success of his African work. He was rewarded by promotion to the Embassy at Pekin, a position in which full success may have been impossible to any one, though some of Macdonald's critics say that a man more experienced in the methods of Chinese and Russian diplomacy would have had a better chance. At any rate, this case illustrates the danger of rewarding success in African administration by promotion to diplomatic duties, which call for different qualities and training.

The separation of the management of East Africa from the ordinary work of the Foreign Office is therefore advisable, in the interests both of the country and of the Foreign Office. Upon this supposition it has been proposed to transfer British East Africa to the charge of the Colonial Office. The change appears natural to those who do not realize the difference between a white man's colony and a dependency which is the home of a numerous and inferior race. What would have been the history of India had it been placed under the Colonial Office? and what may not be the history of our African possessions were they placed under the conditions which have made of the government of India the most magnificent achievement of our race? The Foreign Office has probably managed East Africa as economically and as well as any London

THE FUTURE OF BRITISH EAST AFRICA 263

office could have done during the trying times of the transition. The main faults to be found with it have been its inefficient curb on militarism, and its steady defence of agents who have blundered, even when they have expressly disobeyed its orders and wrecked its policy. Loyally to defend servants who have done their best is an absolute necessity in the case of our representatives abroad, whose credit has to be maintained in the eyes of foreigners. They support their men and we have to support ours. But the historic tradition of the Foreign Office unfits it for managing a commercial and administrative service. And this policy in East Africa has been attended with a very unfortunate result. It has disheartened the officials, whose work has been spoiled, to see blunders not only escape censure, but secure rewards that should only have been earned by complete success.

In addition to the need for reforms in our administrative system, we need a fundamental change in policy. Greater efforts should be made to use local men and materials. There had been no systematic attempt to ascertain the economic resources of the country before the arrival of Sir H. Johnston, and even now the funds at his disposal for this purpose are inadequate.

"Hitherto," said Lugard in 1894, and it is still truer to-day, "they [the Germans] have set us an example in the thorough and practical way in which they set about to develop their territories, though, as regards tact with the natives, the advantage, perhaps, lies with us. Even so much as three years before it was administered, preliminary expeditions of experts and scientists were sent to German East Africa (in 1885) to report on the geology, climate, soil, and vegetation, and this was immediately followed by the establishment of plantations, so that some thirty were in existence in 1888."

Even more important than the discovery of the available economic products of East Africa is the need for more use of native help in the management of the country.

What success would England have gained in India had we ignored the help of native rulers? In the civilization of British East Africa, the more intelligent races can give invaluable assistance. The native merchants of the coast towns can conduct a profitable trade where no European could pay his expenses. For some considerable time to come trade with the less accessible portions of British East Africa must be left to native caravans. In this method of business the Arabs and Suahili are experts. Their assistance is indispensable for the commercial development of the country.

It may be urged that any alliance with the Arabs would be immoral, as their passion for slave-raiding is ineradicable. As the slave business was profitable, and the Arabs do not regard it as objectionable, no doubt they would engage in it if they could do so safely.

THE FUTURE OF BRITISH EAST AFRICA

But the East Coast Arabs and Suahili are sufficiently intelligent to appreciate the benefits of a European connection. "We are children, you are men," said to me Omari Hamadi, the former commander of the Witu army. The leading natives on the coast are eager for European help, and will make sacrifices to secure it. The loyal assistance given by the Lewali of Melindi is an instance of the native readiness to co-operate with the British administrators. But to secure the continued help of the natives they must be fairly treated. They will not help if their religion is to be officially attacked, if their sentiments are to be outraged by proposals to declare polygamy illegal and all children of concubines illegitimate, and if their trade is to be harassed by finicking regulations.

In many provinces of British East Africa there were chiefs ready to support us with their power and influence in the management of the country. Kabarega in Unyoro, Gabriel in Uganda, and Mbaruk of Gazi may be quoted as examples of natives who were willing to help us. But what encouragement did they meet? Kabarega is a political prisoner in Somali-land, practically because he helped his people to resist being placed in bondage to their hereditary foes. Gabriel is an outlaw. Mbaruk of Gazi, in spite of loyal service to the British and a consuming anxiety for peace, has been driven into rebellion and chased with his people into German territory; his alternative was the dishonourable surrender of a kinsman, whose sin was resistance to an admittedly unjust decree.

When the British Government began the administration of British East Africa, in 1895, the greatest need of the country was peace. The protection of the weaker tribes against the tyranny of the strong was the most immediate necessity. Peace has been secured by a series of sanguinary wars, but it seems to have been at length obtained. The Pokomo are now secure from Somali and Suahili raids; the Wakamba can till the plains and valleys around their hills; the Masai are being trained as police to protect the people they once pillaged. We have done our first duty:—

> "Make ye sure to each his own,
> That he reap where he hath sown.
> By the peace among your peoples let men know ye serve the Lord."

We have now to apply the second of the two principles to which our Empire owes its success. Sir Alfred Milner, in his *England in Egypt*, remarks that "the true nature of British influence is a weight, and a decisive weight, cast into the right scale, in the struggle of the better elements of Egyptian society against the worse." It should be the aim of British policy that this definition could be truly applied to our influence throughout our African territories. Kabarega, king of Unyoro; Mbaruk, the chief of Gazi; Selim Bey, the defender of the Equatorial Provinces against the

THE FUTURE OF BRITISH EAST AFRICA 267

Mahdists, are representatives of the best and most intelligent classes in the East African population. But the fate of these men shows that we have not yet learnt how to make the best use of the better element in East African society. Pulteney's pacification of Southern Unyoro, Lugard's defence of Uganda, Ainsworth's management in Ukambani, and the invaluable assistance rendered to the British East Africa Company by the Lewali of Melindi and Mombasa show what excellent results may be obtained by co-operation with the native leaders, if efforts be made to educate them into usefulness, and not to crush them into impotence.

Therefore, the main requirement for that successful administration of British East Africa is a government that will curb militarism, raise a permanent trained staff of men whose hearts are in their work, scientifically develop the natural resources of the country, and enlist the sympathetic co-operation of the better elements in the native population. But successful administration will not alone save East Africa. It will give the country peace and security and prosperity; but these benefits will be half wasted unless they be used as a basis for further progress by a patient and practical philanthropy, and by a tolerant missionary enterprise working in accordance with Christ's command, " Into whatsoever house ye enter, first say, 'Peace be to this house.' "

INDEX

Albert Nyanza, 13
  Discovered by Baker, 79
Arab Explorers, 45

Baker, Samuel, 78, 79, 104
Bantu Tribes, 18, 108
Belesoni Canal, 135
British East Africa Company, 5, 123
  and slavery, 131, 150
  and Witu, 134
  and Germany, 132
  and the Mazrui, 150
  and Lugard, 175
Burton, Sir Richard, 53
  and Nile Sources, 72

Catholic Missionaries, 119, 250
Colvile, Gen. Sir Henry, 212
Congo Free State, 125
Cooley's Criticisms, 67

Denhardt, 45

Economic Value of British East Africa, 238
Emin Pasha, 169, 187
Equatorial Africa, Early Exploration of, 28
European Expedition into British East Africa, The First, 59

Fischer's, Dr. G. A., Expedition, 82
Foreign Office Rule, 246, 260
French, The, in East Africa, 221
Frere, Sir Bartle, 69

Galla, The, 22
Geography of British East Africa, 3, 27
German Aggression, 137
  Treaty with Uganda, 172
Germany and Zanzibar, 126
  and Witu, 134
Grant, 74

Hannington, Bishop, 121
Hardinge, Sir A., 149, 151, 244

Kalema, King of Uganda, 163, 168
Kapti Plains, 10
Karagwe, People of, 75
Kavirondo, The natives of, 21
Kikuya Country, 90
Kilima Njaro, 60
Kirk, Sir John, 128
Krapf, Dr. Ludwig, 53
  and the Galla, 55
  at Mombasa, 55
  translations into Suahili, 56
  and Rebmann, 56, 70
  and Inland Missions, 59

INDEX

Krapf, Dr. Ludwig, *continued*.
  and the Wa-Kamba, 61
  and Methodist Mission, 65
  criticism of, 68

Livingstone, 67, 74
  and Stanley, 106
Lothaire, Major, 167
Lugard, Gen. F. D., 173, 174
  first visit to Uganda, 177
  joins British East Africa Company, 175
  and religious disputes, 181, 191
  and Selim Bey, 184, 210
  war in Uganda, 194

Mackay, A. M., 118, 169
Mackenzie, George S., 130, 147, 244
Masai, The, 20, 82
  and Thomson, 86
  and Carl Peters, 140
Mazrui, The, 144
  Cause of Rebellion, 149
  Commencement of, 152
  end and result of, 161
Mbaruk of Gazi, 146, 150, 152, 156, 265
Missions, 18, 48, 53, 65, 104, 114, 125, 148, 162, 169, 170, 179, 248
Mombasa, 145, 241
Mtesa, King of Uganda, 77, 110
  and Christianity, 114, 120
  Death of, 121
Mwanga, King of Uganda, 121, 162, 164, 168, 194, 219

Natives of British East Africa, 17
New, Charles, 66
  and Mbaruk, 146
  Ascent of Kilima Njaro, 67
Nile, The Sources of the, 31, 71, 78, 80, 125

Pearson, Col., Expedition against Mbaruk, 160
" Periplus of the Red Sea, The," 49
Peters, Dr. Carl, 138, 171
Physical Geography of British East Africa, 6
Portal, Sir Gerald, 200
Portuguese and East Africa, 43
Ptolemy's account of the Coast of East Africa, 33
Pulteney, Major, 216
Pygmies, 23

Rebmann, 56
  and Inland Missions, 59
  return home, 69
Rift Valley, 11, 84, 93

Sanson d'Abbeville's Map, 48
Selim Bey, 186, 206
Shimba Expedition, 159
Slavery, 105, 131, 149, 175, 257
  and Lugard, 175
Soudanese Mutiny, 226
Speke, John Hanning, 72
  Discovery of Victoria Nyanza, 73
  Second Expedition with Grant, 74
  and the Karagwe People, 75

INDEX 271

Speke, John Hanning, *continued.*
  journey to Uganda, 77
  and Mtesa, 111
Stanley, H. M., 106
  and the slave trade, 107
  and Uganda, 109
  and Mtesa, 112
  translation of Scriptures, 115
  first journey across Africa, 124
  Congo Free State, 125
Stokes, 164
  and Mwanga, 167
  and Lugard, 180
Suahili, The, 19, 157
Szek's, Teleki von, Expedition, 89
  and the Kikuya, 91
  and Lake Samburu, 94

Takaunga Dispute, 150
Thomson's, Joseph, Expedition, 84
Thruston, 247
Tucker, Bishop, 179

Uganda, 12
  visited by Speke and Grant, 77
  German Road to, 81
  Arab Traders' route, 81
  Stanley's visit to, 109
  Government under Mtesa, 113
  as a mission field, 116
  Catholic missionaries, 119
  and Mwanga, 121
  and Carl Peters, 138, 171
  Rebellion of Christians and Mohammedans, 163
  and Kiwewa, 163
  Treaty with Germany, 172

Uganda, *continued.*
  under British protection, 173
  and British East Africa Company, 173
  entered by Lugard, 177
  religious difficulties, 181
  Sir William Mackinnon, 189
  War breaks out, 194
  and Foreign Office, 199
  Sir Gerald Portal's Report, 200
  Lord Rosebery and, 200
  Sir J. R. L. Macdonald, 205
  Arrest of Selim Bey, 207
  Revolt in Western, 221
  and the French, 221
  "Pearl of Africa," 239
  Railway, 239
  Unyoro Campaign, 213

Van Höhnel, 89
Vasco da Gama's Expedition, 38
Victoria Nyanza, discovery of, 73
  Thomson's Expedition, 88
  explored by Stanley, 107

Waganda, The, 19
Wahuma, The, in Uganda, 109
Wakefield, 66
Williams, Capt., 189
Wissmann, Lieut., 138
Witu, 133
  Massacre of German Traders in, 141
  Rebellion, 142

Zanzibar and Germany, 127
  and British East Africa Company, 129